ON INCEST

ON INCEST

Psychoanalytic Perspectives

edited by

Giovanna Ambrosio

A Volume in the Psychoanalysis & Women Series
for the Committee on Women and Psychoanalysis
of the International Psychoanalytical Association

KARNAC
LONDON   NEW YORK

First published in 2005 by
H. Karnac (Books) Ltd.
6 Pembroke Buildings, London NW10 6RE

British Library Cataloguing in Publication Data

A C.I.P. for this book is available from the British Library

  ISBN 1 85575 362 6

Edited, designed and produced by The Studio Publishing Services Ltd,
Exeter EX4 8JN

Printed in Great Britain by Hobbs the Printers Ltd

10 9 8 7 6 5 4 3 2 1

www.karnacbooks.com

CONTENTS

FOREWORD

This book contains some of the papers presented at the European Conference on the theme of incest that, as European co-chair of the IPA Committee on Women and Psychoanalysis, I had the priviledge to organize in Ravello, Italy, on the 28 and 29 April 2003; in particular, the papers of Simona Argentieri, Monique Cournut-Janin, Estela Welldon and Juan Eduardo Tesone, analysts who are especially interested in themes such as gender identity, perversions, and incest. Contributions by two other colleagues who took part in the Conference have been added to these papers: the chairperson of COWAP Mariam Alizade, who is the author of many works on feminine identity, and the British psychoanalyst Brendan MacCarthy, who has carried out much theoretical and clinical work on the theme of incest. Both authors present an account of the discussions as they developed during the Conference.

The theme of the Conference was chosen because we noted that, curiously, it has been taken into very little consideration by psychoanalysts during recent years. We wanted to promote a confrontation between past and present, and a clinical and theoretical reflection on a problem that, on account of recent historical, social, and cultural development, seems to contain a special kaleidoscopic quality.

From our perspective, incest is distinct from sexual abuse outside of the family nucleus; incest, of course, includes abuse, but
with a different and particular connotation. At the call for papers
presenting clinical cases of incest for the workshop discussions,
many colleagues with long-standing experience proposed material
that regarded molestation and violence outside the family nucleus.
This called my attention to, and strengthened my conviction about,
the need to gather together the threads of psychoanalytic thinking
in an attempt to foster a clearer conceptualization of what we really
mean when referring to incest, while keeping a careful watch over
the different psychopathological frameworks and various transferential configurations in which we may find ourselves in these cases.
We have also tried to distinguish incestuous "fantasies" from real,
acted out incest.

On the subject of this dramatic theme, you will also find in this
book an attentive view of the "feminine" universe, freed from the
Freudian vision of masochistic passivity and fully restored to the
area of drives.

I wish to thank all those who have agreed to contribute to this
book, thus allowing us to reflect on incest yesterday and today with
the hope that these discussions may stimulate and reinforce theoretical and clinical interest in such a crucial theme.

A special thank you also to Jacqueline Amati Mehler, for her
constant help and for preventing what could have been "lost in
translation".

Giovanna Ambrosio
Editor

CONTRIBUTORS

Giovanna Ambrosio is a full member of the Italian Psycho-analytical Association (AIPsi), the International Psychoanalytical Association, and the Secretary of the Italian Psychoanalytical Association (AIPsi). She is also the Chief Editor of the journal *Psicoanalisi*, and European co-chair of the Committee on Women and Psychoanalysis (2001–2005). Her main scientific interests include the field of the intra-psychic interaction between "the truth and the false", the meanings of "lies" and issues related to the well-known problem of the "confusion of tongues".

Alcira Mariam Alizade, MD, is a psychiatrist and training analyst of the Argentine Psychoanalytic Association. She is current overall chair of the IPA Committe on Women and Psychoanalysis (2001–2005) and former COWAP Latin-American co-chair (1998–2001). Her publications include: *Feminine Sensuality* (Karnac, 1992); *Near Death: Clinical Psychoanalytical Studies* (Amorrortu, Buenos Aires, 1995); *Time for Women* (Letra Viva, Buenos Aires, 1996); *The Lone Woman* (Lumen, Buenos Aires, 1999); *Positivity in Psychoanalysis* (Lumen, Buenos Aires, 2002). She is the editor of IPA–COWAP–Karnac Series (*The Embodied Female, Studies on Femininity, Masculine*

Scenarios) and of the collected papers of COWAP Latin-American *Intergenerational Dialogues* (Lumen, Buenos Aires).

Simona Argentieri is Training and Supervising Analyst of the Italian Psychoanalytical Association (AIPsi) and of the International Psychoanalytical Association. Her main scientific interests are the mind–body relationship, psychosomatic medicine, and the gender identity, on which she has written extensively. In addition to her full-time clinical practice, she has been involved in the field of bio-ethics, in teaching at universities, and in active psychoanalytic divulgation in the mass media. She has dedicated much thought to the relationship between psychoanalysis, culture, and art, particularly the cinema. She is the author of many essays and books on the above subjects. She edited the Italian edition of *Freud and the Art*, and has co-authored: *Freud in Hollywood*; *The Babel of the Unconscious* (on the mother tongue and foreign languages in the psychoanalytic dimension); *Anna Freud, the Daughter*; *The Bogyman* (a small catalogue of infantile anxieties), *The Weariness of Growing Up: Anorexia and Bulimia in a Confused Epoch*; and *The Maternal Father*.

Monique Cournut-Janin is a psychiatrist and a training analyst of the Société Psychanalytique de Paris (SPP). She is a former coordinator of the Jean Favreau Consultation and Treatment Centre. In addition to her work as present training secretary of the SPP, she is a consultant member of the COWAP. Among other texts, she has written *Féminin et Féminité*, published (in French) in Paris by the Presses Universitaires de France (1998).

Brendan MacCarthy was a consultant child psychiatrist at the Tavistock and Portman Clinics in London between 1969 and 1987. He is a member, Training Analyst, and Child Analyst in the British Psychoanalytical Society. He was a Medical Director of the London Clinic of Psychoanalysis 1985–1993 and 1998–2000, and the President of the British Psychoanalytic Society 1993–1996.

Juan Eduardo Tesone completed his psychoanalytic training at the Société Psychanalytique de Paris, of which he became a member in 1992. He is also training analyst of the Argentinian Psychoanalytic Association and of the International Psychoanalytical

Association. He has worked as psychiatrist at the Hôpital de l'Assistance Publique in Paris (1978–1988), psychiatrist at the Direction des Affaires Sanitaires et Sociales de Paris, Departement de l'Enfance et l'Adolescence (1981–1987), and Medical Director of the Centre Médico Psycho-Pédagogique E. Pichon Rivière de Paris (1987–1997). In 1989 he was counsellor at the Ministère des Affaires Sociales de France. In 1997 he returned to Argentina where he currently practises. He is author of over fifty articles in specialized journals in English, French, Italian, German, Serbo-Croat, and Spanish, and co-author of three books published in Italy, Croatia, and Argentina. He teaches at the University of Paris VI and at the UCES in Buenos Aires.

Estela V. Welldon works in private practice as a psychoanalytical psychotherapist, and is an Honorary Consultant Psychiatrist in Psychotherapy at the Portman Clinic, part of the Tavistock Portman NHS Clinics. She is the Founder and ex-Director of the Diploma Course in Forensic Psychotherapeutic Studies at the University College London, and Founder and Honorary Elected Honorary President for Life of the International Association for Forensic Psychotherapy. A Member of the British Association for Psychotherapy and Member and teaching staff of the Institute of Group Analysis and of the International Association of Group Psychotherapy, she was awarded an Honorary Doctor of Science at the Oxford Brook University in 1997 for her contribution to the field of forensic psychotherapy. She acts as an expert in criminal and family law courts. She is also an organizational consultant, consultant to the media, and to film scripts. She is the author of many publications, including *Mother, Madonna, Whore: The Idealization and Denigration of Motherhood* (1988), *Sadomasochism* (2002), in the series of Ideas in Psychoanalysis, published by Icon Books UK and Totem Books USA, and the main editor of *A Practical Guide to Forensic Psychotherapy*, published by Jessica Kingsley in 1997.

Introduction[1]

Giovanna Ambrosio

A new motto: "What has been done to you, poor child?"[2]
Sigmund Freud to Wilhelm Fliess, 22 December 1897

We know how intensely Freud worked around the key issue of trauma and seduction, and how its development—present in all his work and parallel to his clinical experience—came to constitute a basic element for the construction of the metapsychological edifice. We naturally have in mind his fundamental "discovery" of fantasy and, thus, of the centrality of psychic reality. Following this thread of thought, one can appreciate its extension to the whole Freudian corpus, as well as the complexity of its vicissitudes, by no means linear, but rather a source of suffering right from the very early years of its elaboration. On 21 September 1897, Freud wrote to his friend Fliess, "I no longer believe in my neurotica [theory of the neuroses] [. . .] so that one cannot distinguish between the truth and fiction that is cathected with affect" (Freud, 1887–1904, pp. 264–265).

In 1905 Freud was already regretting that he had exaggerated the frequency and the importance of the effects of seduction in

1

children. In 1914d, in "On the history of the psycho-analytic move-ment", Freud wrote regarding infantile sexuality:

> Influenced by Charcot's view of the traumatic origin of hysteria, one was readily inclined to accept as true and aetiologically signifi-cant the statements made by patients in which they ascribed their symptoms to passive sexual experiences in the first years of child-hood—to put it bluntly, to seduction. When this aetiology broke down under the weight of its own improbability and contradiction in definitely ascertainable circumstances, the result at first was helpless bewilderment. Analysis had led back to these infantile sexual traumas by the right path, and yet they were not true. The firm ground of reality was gone. (. . .) the new fact which emerges is precisely that they create such scenes in *phantasy*, and this psy-chical reality requires to be taken into account *alongside* practical reality. [Freud, 1914d, p. 17, my italics]

However, in the "Introductory lectures on psycho-analysis" (Freud, 1916–17, p. 370), when speaking about the "uncanny" frequency of sexual abuse perpetrated on children, Freud seemed to consider in a joint manner the importance of the fantasy of being seduced, but also the real memories of seduction ("so often they are not phantasies but real memories"). He adds that it is not appro-priate to presume that abuse of a child belongs entirely to the realm of phantasy, referring to the clinical cases of certain colleagues in which "such events were real and could be unimpeachably estab-lished . . .".

Finally, in "Moses and monotheism", Freud defined the trauma thus:

> We give the name of traumas to those impressions, experienced early and later forgotten, to which we attach such great importance in the aetiology of the neuroses. [. . .] All these traumas occur in early childhood up to about the fifth year [. . .] it cannot be deter-mined with certainty how long after birth this period of receptivity begins. [. . .] These three points—the very early appearance of these experiences . . ., the fact of their being forgotten and their sexual-aggressive content—are closely interconnected. The traumas are either experiences on the subject's own body or sense perceptions, mostly of something seen and heard—that is *experiences or impres-sions*. [Freud, 1939a, pp. 72, 74, my italics]

Also, Sandor Ferenczi, in his fundamental, classic essay "The confusion of tongues between the adult and the child (1932)—a cornerstone for all of us regarding this theme—was at pains to strongly emphasize the situations in which seduction really took place:

> The real rape of girls who have hardly grown out of the age of infants, similar sexual acts of mature women with boys, and also enforced homosexual acts, are more frequent occurrences than has hitherto been assumed. [Ferenczi, 1932, p. 227]

We are not going to pursue here the whole course of Freud's reflections and doubts on the theme of trauma, seduction, and fantasy; Phyllis Greenacre has skilfully guided us through this enterprise in a 1967 paper. Nor are we going to deal exhaustively with the clinical, theoretical debate arising from the trauma–seduction, reality–fantasy issue—an issue that, unfortunately, has not spared us from becoming the bored witnesses of squalid instrumental gossip.

What I think is important, and is present within Freudian thinking, is the centrality of psychic reality *alongside* (Freud, 1914d) affective reality; and also that traumas are to be considered as *experiences or impressions* (Freud, 1939a).

I intend to present the theme of really acted out incest, distinguishing it from incestuous fantasies. As psychoanalysts, and thanks to our metapsychological know-how enriched by the post-Freudians—Klein, Winnicott, Rosenfeld, Bion, Bleger, Greenacre, Loch, Gaddini, and Green, to mention only a few of the most significant authors—today we possess the tools that will allow us to access and explore, together with our patients, remote internal landscapes.

I think it is hazardous not to distinguish between fantasy and reality, especially when it regards the possibility of helping a patient. This would be confusing when confronting the psychopathological picture of a person, together with his/her psychic structure, defences, and mechanisms of functioning. Moreover, this lack of distinction between fantasy and reality would inevitably have serious consequences on the transference relationship. On this point I wholly agree with Estela Welldon when she states at the beginning of her chapter in this book that: "The importance of the *reality* of family dynamics in incest can hardly be overstressed, but somehow this has not always been acknowledged, since it was shadowed by a marked adherence to the seduction theory with its emphasis on unconscious fantasies.".

Welldon appropriately quotes Brendan MacCarthy (1982): "I think it is a criticism of the contribution of Psychoanalysis to Psychiatry and allied professions that locating the theme of incest in the world of unconscious fantasy deflected attention away from the reality of incest and delayed the discovery of sexual abuse within the family."

Notwithstanding that the centrality of fantasy in the theory of trauma has been a basic assumption in the entire set-up of psycho-analytic theory, this does not authorize us to lose sight of or, worse still, deny those situations in which the reality of the trauma emerges in all its crudeness as an act that "really" happened, and these are situations that confront us with very particular psychic and psychopathological vicissitudes, each marked by its own speci-ficity.

It would seem to be a kind of psychoanalytic "abuse" to put our interpretative tools at the service of the denial of reality by presum-ing, as good "politically-correct" analysts, that what counts is only the fantasy. The unfortunate consequence would be the denial of an incestuous reality that, the more it were denied, the greater would be its effect on the quality of the transference, thus creating the conditions and the space for an eventual destructive drifting towards an erotic quality.

Again I quote from Phyllis Greenacre's (1967) thoughts when she reflects on trauma:

> It is my opinion that, in situations when obvious traumatic experi-ences are associated with the underlying fantasies, the mnestic trace that is left behind—the imprint—is more intense and the tendency to fixation can be greater than in cases in which the experiences have been more bland and have been of an accidental character. [Greenacre, 1967, p. 299, Italian original, my translation]

She continues:

> [. . .] On the basis of my experience, however, I still think that in cases in which an actual seduction has occurred, and above all in

cases in which it has been repeated, the child has less sense of being able to control what happens than is true in cases when the situation, as a whole, remains confined within the child's fantasy. He knows that the fantasy is his own production . . . [Greenacre, 1967, p. 303, Italian original, my translation]

Countertransference problems in the feminine dimension

Before presenting a brief examination of the works published in this book, I should like to dwell on an exquisitely clinical aspect regarding cases of really acted out incest: the countertransference and, more specifically, a complex countertransference condition that, in my experience, has been activated with women patients who have been the victims of maternal incest.

In recent years there have been many important psychoanalytic contributions on "the feminine", aimed at finally liberating the female figure from the mortifying Freudian triad of "masochism, passivity, narcissism". In particular, the incestuous situation puts us dramatically face to face with the whole possible range of feminine psychopathology. We are confronted with an image—in this case pitiless—of responsible subjectivity: as Simona Argentieri rightly says in Chapter One: "women . . . are by now recognized as being the protagonists of, and therefore responsible for, the whole range of sexual and aggressive drives, both in a horizontal direction towards men, and in a vertical direction in the parent–child relationship."

When talking about molestation and incest within the family nucleus, the fantasy is usually organized in the masculine dimension; but, with increasing frequency, in my clinical work I come across incestuous situations organized in the feminine dimension and, from the clinical, psychopathological, and transferential viewpoint, I find that these situations are the most insidious and difficult to handle in the transference.

The experience that has stimulated these reflections refers particularly to incestuous relationships between mothers and daughters, sometimes, but not always, with a male figure as a "vector" in situations still far away from any oedipal triangulation. Naturally, I am not talking about differences in the quality and the intensity of the trauma (this depends on the combination of infinite variables about which we cannot make any kind of generalization); but I am talking about the clinical sensation of having greater difficulty in coming into contact with these "violations in the feminine" and of subtracting them from the defensive mechanisms of denial, splitting, and isolation that in these situations seem to me to be especially violent and tenacious.

I would like to mention three aspects that appeared to me to be like the dangerous Sirens encountered by Ulysses:

1.   The state of "extreme" need (marked by an apparently special urgency when compared with other patients) as an *instrument of seduction in the transference* (and not only as the sign of an authentic need for maternal preoccupation and caring). It would appear that only by guaranteeing for themselves the perpetuation of the emergency and of the unconditioned availability of the analyst, can these patients feel really loved. The request that reaches the analyst—often a genuine dictatorial claim—appears to be that of total abnegation in respect to their needs in the form of a request to form a couple that is maniacalized *by* and *in* the emergency.

2.   Incest as the conveyer of an evil and weighty "secondary advantage of the illness", as though *perpetuating the illusion of possessing the lost object*. From this arises a violent and sometimes unsustainable feeling of incompleteness—a kind of tragic destiny from which one will never be able to escape— that, in accordance with the different psychopathological configurations, sometimes reveals itself through fantasies about the body.

     This continually presents us with a difficult situation in the transference–countertransference relationship. On the part of the patient *the analyst* is seen as a non-incestuous object, therefore as a violently *frustrating* object because—by not giving in to fusional seduction, often characterized by a very high degree of eroticizing sensuality—he/she does not support the omnipotent illusion and does not restore the lost object. The analyst has difficulty in moving acrobatically between the necessary function of disillusion and the equally necessary need to support a quota of illusion at the service of the sense of self, continually moving with extreme caution within a sensorial *scenario* that is at boiling point. Within this difficult transferential situation, what is inserted in the relationship with the analyst is the theme of the *betrayal* of the incestuous mother–"lover". Some patients ask themselves: what would be the benefits of analysis if the analyst does not guarantee the restoration of the missing piece and is therefore a source of disillusion, while one word from the incestuous object is enough to infuse a feeling of happy serenity?

3.   The emergence of a pathological quality, specific to these cases, that seems to consist of a kind of *"greediness for an oceanic feeling"* that only the incestuous object can satisfy and appease. The fusional area appears to become almost virulent and obstinately opposes any attempt at objectualization (also represented by the "third" position of the interpreting analyst) in defence of an unbearable separation anxiety ("If I don't sleep in my mother's arms, then I fall to pieces, I die"). Just as though, strengthened and overheated by the incestuous experience, this area could constitute a kind of white-hot explosive material, ready to spread out before any little step towards integration and the object.

The oedipal crossroads

The works published in this book—more or less in agreement with each other—seem to focus on two points of great interest. One revolves around the oedipal and pre-oedipal events, and the other concerns a background theme of no less importance: how have our patients changed during the last twenty years, but, especially, how have we analysts changed (Gaddini, 1984).

The work by Simona Argentieri, in particular, deals with the theme of incest from the point of view of psychoanalytic theory and practice, and begins by examining the various biological and social-anthropological theories. Distinguishing incest from abuse and incestuous fantasies from really acted out incest, Argentieri goes beyond the phenomenic ground and analyses both the conscious and unconscious levels that lead an individual to practise incest, as well as the damage that incest inflicts on the development process.

For this purpose, she dwells on the differences between the different psychoanalytic theoretic models, emphasizing the complexity of the question relative to incest and to the relationship between pre-oedipal and oedipal levels.

The essential point, and also the most difficult, says Argentieri, is not to anchor one's thought (and the patient) to one level of development only, but also to try to take into consideration the fact that the most archaic defensive functioning and mechanisms have in any case passed through the oedipal crossroads, deforming it and being in their turn transformed. Argentieri points out how one of the most devastating aspects is the consequent lack of intrapsychic and interpersonal distinction between the tender and sensorial aspects and the erotic drive aspects.

In the last part of her work, beginning with an observation about social–cultural change, she focuses her attention on how the defences change: from the register of repression to that of splitting and denial and, even more, to the ambiguous boundary with so-called normality and with the very early defensive organizations of non-integration and ambiguity—a condition in which the Oedipus is heavily penalized by the pre-oedipal defences. In this context of tendential defensive regression towards undifferentiation, in which the oedipal knot seems to be loosened, if not eluded, Argentieri wonders whether it can happen that incest, too, provokes less anguish, less guilt, less horror, but not less damage.

Along these same lines of thought, Juan Tesone believes that incest does not become inscribed in the linear continuation of the Oedipus complex. On the contrary, within the serious psychopathological configuration of the incestuous family, a massive attack is produced on the oedipal triangulation. Differently from the Oedipus that links desire to the symbolic law, thus permitting the emergence of alterity, incest cancels the boundaries between members of the family and introduces confusion among them. *Eros* is put at the service of *Thanatos*; it provokes a traumatic effraction in the psychic life of the child who is the object of incest, thus generating a state of de-structuring and, therefore, annihilating congelation of psychic life. The prohibition of incest, states Tesone, is not founded on moral precepts; it is universal and includes all cultures. It is the guarantor of the psychic constitution of the human being, and regulates the laws of social exchange. Tesone wonders whether the horror of the incestuous act is due solely to the transgression of the prohibition of incest, or whether it does not, at the same time, include the transgression of the narcissistic taboo that thus multiplies its devastating effect.

Monique Cournut-Janin also puts the problem of incest into the Freudian theoretic and metapsychological framework, emphasizing the importance of the vicissitudes of perverse polymorphic organization that characterizes infantile sexuality and is destined to be more or less subject to re-activation according to life events. This sexuality, subject to secondary repression at the end of the oedipal period, has the effect of permitting "normally neurotic future parents to not be able to see or hear the incestuous sexuality of their infant . . ." (p. 73, this volume). This happens, of course, if there are no serious parental pathologies.

Cournut-Janin then examines the different possibilities of incest according to the protagonists—father–daughter, father–son, mother–son, mother–daughter—beginning with a reference to the well-known case of Katharina (Freud, 1892–95). She enriches her reflections with some clinical vignettes taken from her experience as a psychotherapist at a Reception Centre for teenagers with problems. She pays particular attention to incest between mother and daughter, defining it as "the most archaic". She distinguishes *femininity* from *feminine*. The former refers back to a complicity handed down from mother to daughter; it presupposes a situation of three, and is organized in the name of the father and of men. The feminine, on the other hand, is more profound and secret, transmitted from woman to woman in the guise of femininity. And it is here that, for the daughter, her destiny can run aground. The originary love, "the love of the mother, the love for the mother, the love body-to-body, mouth-to-mouth, orifice-to-orifice" (p. 77, this volume), can be fixed in this archaic form and no longer evolve. The adult woman tosses about in an archaic world in which every opportunity for separation is excluded.

In line with the other authors who have contributed to this volume, Cournut-Janin sees the incestuous situation as a drama in which the destruction of the other and of the difference takes place.

From a different viewpoint, Estela Welldon shows us how a psychoanalyst can put his/her mental functioning and the "tools of the trade" at the service of situations that are not specifically psychoanalytic—i.e. situations of group therapy—and how one can "think" psychoanalytically in situations different from the setting and from the analytic dyad.

The significance of Welldon's work rests on the clinical wealth of her experience, on confronting in the same therapeutic work group "both victims and perpetrators of incest together but not related", with great attention to penetrating the interwoven and sometimes inauspicious family relationships. Particular mention is made of the "secrecy" that surrounds incest and this is singled out as "the core of the situation"; every family member is always involved in this business of "not saying". From this point of view, the author suggests that incest corresponds to the effort to "keep the family together".

As always, Welldon, who is the author of an important text, *Mother, Madonna, Whore* (1988), is very aware of the feminine universe and, therefore, of feminine perversions: "Jocasta was far better equipped, even consciously, to recognize Oedipus as her son . . .". Starting with some clinical cases of incest in which women were either the perpetrators or the victims, she explores the psychic vicissitudes and the defence organizations, with particular attention to the transference and countertransference. The advantage of the therapeutic group is that it acts as the container for mirroring experiences between perpetrators and victims and therapeutically promotes the relationship with the others.

> Group analytical psychotherapy can become, if well administered, the best form of treatment for victims and perpetrators of incest since they share, by nature of their predicament, a history of an engulfing, intense, inappropriate, distorted, physical, and sexual relationship of a highly secretive type within the family situation [. . .] Group analytical therapy breaks through patterns of self-deception, fraud, secrecy, and collusion thatare invariably present in these cases. [Welldon, this volume, p. 94]

Thus, we find ourselves faced with a choice that cannot be considered only technical, but clinical and, therefore, theoretical. In fact, while it is true that the therapeutic group administered by a psychoanalyst—in the way that Estela Welldon has described—offers a precious experience of mirroring between perpetrators and victims, it is equally true that the analytic relationship, the setting, and the "analysing situation" (Donnet, 2002) remains a kind of experience that is unique and irreplaceable.

On this point, and in accordance with other authors, perhaps it would be necessary when speaking of incest to think of it within a psychoanalytic relationship. Clinical experience indicates that what seemed to be a pre-condition, at the service of the patient's needs, was the setting; that special container in which to relive the experience of the horror of incest, introducing it first of all into the transference communication through the use of our specific tools— beginning with the fundamental work of resignification of archaic elements in forms relative to more evolved phases of development such as the *Nachträglichkeit*—but especially through working continually *on* and *with* our countertransference, while at the same time remaining closely attentive to the possible collusion of the couple, to the seduction of ambiguity and to the undifferentiated symmetry that are intrinsic to the nature of the incestuous trauma. So, why not try to think of the group possibly as a propaedeutic synergic relationship, rather than as an alternative to the analytic relationship?

The work of Mariam Alizade, "Incest: the damaged psychic flesh" (Chapter Five), introduces a particular point of view. Starting with a clinical vignette, she presents her reflection on a case of "verbal incest". Moving away from the basic hypothesis that we have assumed here, she suggests the possibility—as far as the psychic vicissitudes linked to the incestuous trauma are concerned—of thinking of the *really acted* as being superimposed on the *really said*. Here we are again confronted with the relationship between reality and fantasy, between the effects that verbal threats or enacted threats can have, on account of the psychic and psychopathologic vicissitudes.

The author also distinguishes between the various degrees of pathogenesis resulting from incest. She invites us not to "put all incest in the same basket", and draws attention to the importance of the many "psychic effects and to the weight of culture, traditions, and habits on the mind at different periods of history". She adds that "Psychoanalysis should work closely and frequently with history in order to appreciate the fact that some psychoanalytic concepts are relative in nature".

She then speaks of a type of incest that she calls "obnoxious", where "the more vulnerable participant, whose consent has at most been minimal, experiences the pleasant effects of seduction together with subsequent confusion". Within this framework, she examines the psychic consequences of this event—first, the damage caused to the symbolic function.

In line with the other authors, Alizade seems to single out in incest a disturbing and disorganizing potentiality regarding the whole psychic metabolism:

> The fact that resolution of the Oedipus complex is consequently impossible means that many patients are overwhelmed by conflictual networks of love and hate, crime and punishment, in a sort of endless pathological spiral that constitutes a barrier to the successful negotiation of the oedipal situation. [Alizade, this volume, p. 110]

Last, but not least, Brendan MacCarthy offers us some precious "counterpoints", almost a condensed picture of this complex issue. The author begins to "see" the incestuous acts as an experience of loss, in which the question should be: "whose body is it anyway?".

Then he goes on to consider this dramatic issue inside the analytic encounter, by emphasizing the importance of the sex of the analyst: "It is a generally held view by analysts, that the sex of the analyst is more or less irrelevant in most cases, but incest victims usually feel very strongly about analyst sex choice" (this volume, p. 117).

The author deals with a crucial problem about ethics and sustains that—in his experience—he has noted "that boundary violations, especially of incest victims, are virtually not represented in more intensive therapies, particularly psychoanalysis", but are much more common in psychotherapeutic treatments at a frequency of one weekly session or less. "The object intermittently seen would seem to be more tantalizing to both parties", liable to establish more dangerous liaisons, while treatments closer to full analysis, in which the transference is central to the work, do not usually lead to abusive situations.

Finally, MacCarthy underlines the importance of thinking about incest tomorrow

> because we need to consider gathering material about completed treatments and follow-up outcome studies. We are living in an era

when evidence-based medicine is demanded everywhere. We cannot just say that we take histories, and we talk about the Oedipus complex, but we don't know what happens, or whether our work leads to long-term benefit. I believe that follow-up will show that for these cases psychoanalytic therapy is far superior to other approaches, including medication. [MacCarthy, this volume, pp. 119–120]

We have briefly mentioned how important it is for us as psychoanalysts to pay close attention to the change in our patients and, naturally, in ourselves. For this reason, and as the contributors to this book have reminded us more or less explicitly, we must observe how this change reverberates on the analytic relationship; in particular on the transference play, on the quality and consistency of the patients' defences, on the "refinement" of our analytic tools, and also on the risks, on our part, of giving in to the enveloping seduction of undifferentiation by colluding with the most deceptive and harmful defences of the patients—first of all, denial.

To my mind, the following are the focal points of the essays contained in this book.

1. The need not to surrender to the seduction of ambiguity and to restore to incest, with its horror, all its specific psychopathological consistency of "sexual violence of an incestuous nature", as Juan Tesone suggests, without confusing it with abuse: a confusion that has perhaps reflected an extreme attempt to defend ourselves from this horror (as, again, Simona Argentieri suggests), but that at the same time risks blurring our vision and making us lose the coordinates in the transference–countertransference relationship, acting upon us like an evil "Sand-man".

2. In cases of really acted incest, the centrality of pre-oedipal vicissitudes and, therefore, the difficult theme of the process of differentiation, separation, and individuation that leads to the possibility of "seeing" the other.

In this perspective, the works contain a central point that is expressed in different ways: the need to accede to the realm of the pre-oedipal, to consider its vicissitudes and the various combinations, and the self, and how they intersect with the oedipal crossroads.

Another fundamental content that is expressed more or less directly in this book is the risk of the confusion of languages in the analytic couple at work. In the incestuous situation this can be organized at the extremes of horror, not only—as is obvious and unfortunately *déjà vu*—through the erotic acting-out in the transference, but also—and this seems to me to be a crucial point, central in Simona Argentieri's work and repeated in that of Juan Tesone—in less visible, more subtle and elusive forms through collusion between Bleger's (1967) ambiguous nucleus of the patient and of the analyst. These are viscous situations dominated by a warm, comfortable, and non-conflictual symmetry between analyst and patient, and what is lost is any principle whatsoever of discernment and of asymmetry. When dealing with cases of patients who have *really* suffered incest, when faced with the horror and the desolation, the lacerations in the web of psychism that I sometimes seem to see in these situations, this para-incestuous relationship would become an evil and iatrogenic situation.

These essays, although they share a minimum of common denominator, also suggest different points of view regarding both theory and clinical methods and technique. This confirms the need to share our reflections on this matter, and to make of our differences a reservoir of enrichment. It certainly seems to me that there remains a very large gap in our necessarily incomplete discussions. What does "pre-oedipal" mean? Which, as Sandler asks, are the implicit theories of each of us? How are the different theories organized in everyday clinical work and in the transference interplay? What differences are there between us regarding these themes? What role does narcissism play? Which is the crossroads between Narcissus and Oedipus, an area towards which Juan Tesone has directed our attention with his reflections? It appears to me that this book has the merit of bringing the theme of incest out of the shadow of scotoma or, worse still, of denial, and of having given it back its name, thus banishing the triumph of euphemistic ambiguity that is unfortunately very widespread today. This has meant trying to restore to this terrible event its own psychopathological specificity, trying to represent its various possible vicissitudes that, beginning from the transference interplay, take shape in the psychic scenario of a patient, both in terms of structure and of defences or defensive mechanisms.

Notes

1. Translated from Italian by Jill Cucco.
2. J. W. Goethe, *La vocazione teatrale di Wilhelm Meister*, 4th Book, the Song of Mignon.

CHAPTER ONE

Incest yesterday and today: from conflict to ambiguity[1]

Simona Argentieri

To which sphere of competence does incest belong? To the sphere of morality, of biology, of psychology, of legislation, of culture . . .? What is certain is that during the course of time and of history, sexual intercourse between blood relations has been the cause of reflection and debate on the part of censors, poets, scientists, ethnologists, sociologists, anthropologists, and psychoanalysts. The common starting point between so many disciplines is that the taboo on incest is universal, although articulated in many complicated variations regarding the degree of relationship; or perhaps—as Demause says—it is incest that is universal and consequently calls for prohibition. The first problem that we have to face, therefore, is taking into account all these different approaches while keeping a clear distinction between the methodologies.

We must also consider that the concept of incest is closely correlated with the equally multi-disciplinary concept of family. As the *Dizionario di Sociologia* (De Marchi, Ellena & Cattarinussi, 1987) says:

> the nuclear family as a group of men, women and children is more or less universal on account of the great adaptive capacities of

human beings. There are no linear evolutionary laws, but alterna-
tions, cycles; there is no ideal static model, but many variations.

From the sociological point of view, therefore, the irreducibility and
the complexity of the phenomenon of family, together with all its
biological, sexual, psychological, economic, religious, and political
aspects, ensure that, because it is so apparently obvious, it is always
the expression of both nature and culture and belongs contempora-
neously to the public as well as to the private sphere. This partly
explains its continuity in time, to the extent that in his *Dizionario
Sociologico*, Gallino states that: "The survival, not the end, of the
family appears to be necessary to the historic development of
democracy".

Incidentally, I think that the way in which we deal with
the concept of family in psychoanalysis requires a certain amount
of caution. Psychoanalysis is not—or at least should not be—
"normative" about the family model. I believe that we must
above all analyse what exists, what persists or changes, how it
changes, and what the consequences are. Instead, there is a strong
tendency in psychoanalysis, in my opinion, to construct patterns
of relationships and models that are absolute; for example, by
speaking of mother or father as fixed stereotypes and superim-
posing levels of role, functions, and gender identity (Argentieri,
1988).

Regarding the problem of exogamy, in accordance with the view
of many sociologists and in contrast with that of certain anthropologists, I think that it is strictly correlated with the problem of
incest but cannot be superimposed on it. If the taboo prohibits
sex between blood relations, then it is not only an exogamic rule;
because exogamy, as well as prohibiting, prescribes the union
outside of the family group. We cannot assume that the destructive effect of incest on the family is the reason for the prohibition;
however, it is certain that incest disarticulates the symbolic network
of family relations. (Even on this assumption there can be discussion, although to us as psychoanalysts it seems obvious. For
example, some people wonder whether the contrary is not the
case; i.e., it is the fact that the taboo exists that renders incest
destructive.)

Theories on the taboo on incest

Let us begin by saying that up until now, no single theory has managed to definitely and exhaustively explain why the taboo on incest, even though in various forms, is universal. The quantity of theories that have been produced (about twenty accredited and many that are bizarre, to say the least) is already a clear indication of this. Even so, I think it would be useful to summarize them briefly.[2]

Biological theories

At the beginning of the last century Hobhouse, Wheeler, and Ginsberg (1915), Lowie (1920) and others considered the taboo itself to be of an instinctive nature. There would be a "natural" and inborn repulsion against sexual intercourse between relatives, as though in the genotype of our species there were a particular gene that produces a behavioural reaction against incest. This idea is not very convincing because, as Freud himself points out, it would not be necessary to threaten such harsh sanctions if the attraction were not so strong.

The eugenic hypothesis is less ingenuous and more substantial, stating that the taboo on incest is a "spontaneous" protection against the damage that can be caused by reproduction between relatives, both by the appearance of recessive hereditary diseases in the homozygosis, as well as for the loss of the advantages of heterozygosis (greater vitality, fertility, longevity, etc.). The eugenic hypotheses are reinforced by arguments from the worlds of animals (weakening through inbreeding) and of plants (Mendel speaks of the thriving characteristics of hybrids, while self-fecundation of plants is considered to be an involutionary process). Darwin says that nature "abhors continued self-fecundation". But, in fact, the scientific elements supporting this are very recent; there are only about twenty hereditary genetic illnesses and the risk of the "taint" are relatively modest. On the other hand, the theories against incest date back to antiquity: from Aristotle, who predicted dire consequences for descent amongst blood relations, to the Romans, who were the first to codify its illegitimacy.

In summary, these observations are non-systematic and, above all, do not make any distinction between sex and reproduction.

These hypotheses—typical "ad hoc theories"—are an example of the defensive use that we can sometimes make of biological explanations in order to support ideologies without having to justify them. This also occurs when "hygienic" justifications are sought for rationalizing rituals such as circumcision or food interdictions of a religious nature. Attempts to find confirmation in the world of the primates are just as deceptive. The theories of Darwin, and after him Freud, on the behaviour of the great African apes were simply wrong. As we are told today by ethologists, the social regulations of the apes, our ancestors, are in reality extremely variable (ranging from solitary animal to family groups, social group, "harem", etc.) and the mother–child couple (pertaining, indeed, to all mammals) is such only until the maturity of the young. Nor can the so-called proto-taboo, that in other species assigns to particular differential signals (smell, song) the task of stimulating sexual attraction only between individuals of other groups, offer more than a generic suggestion to the world of human beings.

Bio-psychological theories

Westermark (1894) believes that, through natural selection, an instinctive lack of erotic attraction develops towards those with whom one has co-habited. This line of thought is followed also by Havelock Ellis (1906), Max Marcuse (1915), and Marvin Harris (1968), all of whom invoke a "bio-psychological" component of the taboo. On the whole, there are more descriptions—contradicted by the facts—than explanations. Moreover, as we have learned from psychoanalysis, there is a substantial difference between lack of attraction and abhorrence; while the distance is minimal between desire and repulsion. Starcke (1889) invoked the disrupting action of incest on the family, and Malinowski (1927) strongly proclaimed the effect of social chaos and the impossibility of transmitting culture from one generation to another. But these are circular propositions, with cause–effect connections that can be overturned; moreover, other family systems could be hypothesized (and, in fact, examples can always be found) that are "compatible" with incestuous practices. Thus, the problem is simply shifted from sexuality on to the family.

Socio-anthropological theories

We only need to make a passing reference to the strange hypothesis of McLennan (1865) according to which the shortage of women within the human horde would lead to the capture of wives from external hordes, and to the well-known theory of Durkheim (1898) that overturns the terms of the problem and considers the taboo a consequence of exogamy. According to this line of thought, totemism would be an obligatory phase of human evolution. The theories "of alliance and exchange" have their precursor in Saint Augustine, and—after Tylor (1888) and Fortune (1932), who emphasize the value of exogamy in promoting cooperation between different families, thus leaving aside the problem of sexuality—we come to the famous conceptualization of Lévi-Strauss that met with such success during the past decades.

The theory of Claude Lévi-Strauss is too complex and too well known for me to try to summarize it. For the purposes of our discourse, I will limit myself to recalling that he overcomes the functional concept and states that the taboo is an ontological category of the human spirit; in his comparison between "language" and exogamy, the prohibition to sexually use the daughter or sister obliges men to give them as wives to other men and, reciprocally, constitutes their own right to women. (As many feminists vehemently noted at the time, women were thus reduced to "gifts" or merely objects of desire or renunciation.) After the world-wide enthusiasm for the structuralism of the recent past, I do not think that his ideas represent for us today anything more than a brilliant metaphor. (We are also indebted to him for the theory on the weakening of desire on account of cohabitation, and I shall return to this theme later.)

The taboo on incest as myth

None of the theories that we have referred to is sufficient to account for the eternal problem of incest, and every one of them (thanks to the careful exploration of anthropologists such as Margaret Mead or Lucy Mair) can be confirmed or refuted according to the variety of human customs throughout time and space. Even the psychoanalytical hypothesis has an implicit conceptual and methodological weakness; we all admit this, beginning with Freud himself.

I do not intend to go through the various stages of Freudian thought, and his hope of being able to base on empirical data the hypothesis that culture is founded on instinctive renunciation, that the taboo is transmitted with onto-philogenetic linearity from generation to generation, and that it resurfaces in a symbolic form in dreams, in delusions and in the fantasies of any human being whatsoever. We can, however, reach a compromise by considering the history of the primitive parricidal and cannibalistic horde that transmits the taboo on incest, with its burden of anxiety and guilt, morality and religion, from one generation to another as a *myth*. This is suggested by Green (1992), who describes the myth in his own way as a kind of "collective transitional object". Moreover, a long time before Green and before psychoanalysis, Sallustio wrote about myths: "These things never happened, but they always exist".

Although we may renounce the "historic truth" of the murderous phratry, certain definite points of reference remain:

- the taboo on incest is universal, as is the violation of this prohibition;
- the family as a structure is also universal, although extremely variable, and within it incest as a taboo and as a violation assumes meaning.

External reality and internal reality

Statistics in a field as elusive as incest are always unreliable. To us, who are more attentive to the deep levels of meaning than to those of overt behaviour, they are of little use; and in our turn we can offer data that are enlightening but difficult to compare with those gathered through other methodologies. Having said this, we must take note of the fact that, according to those who have tried to translate the problem of incest into numbers, as far as I know in first place there is the incest of father with daughter, then brother with sister, brother with younger brother, father with son, and, last, mother with sons and daughters.

How do these statistical data change through time and in different cultures? It appears that progress in the rules of civil cohabitation has led to a decrease in the number of the coarser and more brutal cases of authoritarian, possessive fathers (in Italian, *padre–padrone*), but at the same time to an increase in cases of reporting to the authorities and of no longer keeping things hidden within the family (in Italian, *omertà*—family's silent complicity). But probably other, more subtle, forms proliferate and continue to escape systematic enquiry.[3] (The observations of Estela Welldon (1991) come to mind—to which I shall return later—about the widespread refusal to recognize the problem of incestuous tendencies in mothers.)

From my by now considerable clinical experience, both direct (analyses, psychotherapy, and consultations) and indirect (consultations and supervision of colleagues and students), I have been able to distinguish the following:

- dramatic cases of explicit and consummate incest over a long period of time, undergone by someone who has then come into analysis;
- cases of "soft" incest, masked as ambiguous bodily contacts (the most frequent) reported by those who have committed them and also by those who have been the victims;
- cases of pathological defensive solutions against inhibited incestuous drives and fantasies.

Certainly, from the ethical as well as the legal standpoint, there is a sharp distinction between victim and perpetrator, between sexual violence, plagiary, and abuse, and between someone who has materially carried out the sexual act and someone who has collusively facilitated it. But on the psychological plane, the situation is inevitably much more tormented and elusive. The paradox that differentiates the psychoanalytical approach from that of other disciplines is that, for us, it is very difficult—at least from the genetic viewpoint—to separate the person who is the passive partner from the person who is the active partner in the sexual act; in many cases the person who commits incest has in turn suffered it, and just as frequently the psychopathological distortions that are the cause of incest are spread throughout the whole family group and are the same distortions that the incest then determines in the victim.

> For example, there is case of a woman who, in order to avoid the unwanted sexual attentions of her husband, sent him to sleep in their daughter's room while keeping the younger son with her. Or that of two parents with strongly perverse traits and whose sexuality was characterized by hatred and inhibition, who—especially the mother who needed to enact split-off aspects of herself—encouraged incest between their son and their youngest daughter with the almost explicit message that this was common and "normal" behaviour.

> Another dramatic clinical example was that of a consultation that unfortunately did not lead to a course of therapy. An attractive and intelligent girl aged twenty-four, with a degree in literature and who worked temporarily, had to continue living with her family: upper middle class, cultured, well-off, composed of father, mother, and a brother who was three years older, had interrupted his university studies, and was tyrannical and violent. The brother was systematically physically violent to her and beat her, especially at night, for futile and often non-existent motives. The father pretended not to see, and the mother rebuked her for provoking her brother and for risking upsetting her father if she complained to him. The maximum paradox was when their parents took them on holiday to hotels or holiday villages, and put them in the same bedroom. In the morning when the girl appeared covered in scratches and bruises, the mother would silence her with a glance in case it would look bad in front of the other guests. This young girl was apparently unaware of the sexual problem masked by the physical violence, of the confusion between sexual drives and aggressive sado-masochistic drives; and I am afraid that it was her unconscious complicity with the perverse family fabric that interrupted the analytic project.

We know that an essential turning point occurred in Freud's thought when he understood that being seduced by a parent is a more or less ubiquitous fantasy in the child, and that only in certain single cases is this traumatic seduction experienced in reality.[4] His most important intuition, however, was when he understood that both the fantasy and the real event could have the same pathogenic effect.[5] Furthermore, we know that the same identical childhood dramas can produce both neurotic inhibitions as well as perverse forms of behaviour.

Another obviously important, but also elusive, fact is that of the age at which the incest is committed. In many cultures there is an initial, fairly long period of life during which children of both sexes can freely enjoy intimacy with their mother's body (sometimes also with the father's) without interdiction or conflict; until the time when cultural mores, or the father—if there are fathers—brusquely and peremptorily impose the caesura of separation. (The most impressive example is that of the Japanese tradition in which a little boy can live happily according to his own omnipotent whims or fancies until the age of seven; at that point the child is traumatically torn from intimacy with his mother and from the dimension of *amae*[6] and is entrusted to a harsher discipline.) Perhaps it is this diffused habit of initial "privilege" that has given rise to the fantasy that a historic "pre-human" epoch existed in which incest was possible and pacific. Moreover, Freud observed that kings and queens, demons and gods were exempt from the prohibition of incest, owing to the principle of omnipotence.

The significance of the rule of detachment between mother and son is certainly to avoid incest and to encourage individuation and growth—two aims that evidently coincide. This leads to a reconsideration of the age-old ambiguity according to which intimacy between mother and daughter could continue harmlessly *ad infinitum*, thus implicitly denying feminine instinctuality (Argentieri, 1985).

To return to the manifest problem, we know that, unfortunately, incest can occur at any age—from infancy to latency, to pre-puberty, to puberty, to adolescence, to adulthood—and that, on the whole, the earlier it occurs the more devastating it is, when the damage penetrates into the organization of the structure and of the thought processes, producing the more invalidating defences of splitting and denial (Alvarez, 1992). We should add that the kinship bond of the incestuous couple, from our psychoanalytic viewpoint, is important not so much because of the blood relationship, but because of the degree of intimacy and habit that exists during the growth period. Thus, we must discriminate between the significance of seduction on the part of a stepfather living in the family since the children were young, and seduction by a biological father living far away and seen only occasionally: two situations that are obviously both pathogenous but are governed by different dimensions of trauma and confusion.

As we try to clarify later, in the clinical dimension it is necessary to make further subtle distinctions; for example, the age when incest occurs, as well as the difference in age and in levels of power between the couple. It would also be important (although less important than in other contexts) to establish the type of violence—dramatic or "soft", overt or covert—and the degree of the sexual act, from caresses to complete intercourse. Also the distinction between homosexual and heterosexual incest is not so sharply defined as would appear from the description. As I try to explain further on, we also need to understand what are the underlying unconscious fantasies and, for each of the couple, what is the sense of their own and the other's gender identity.

Last, I think that the specificity of our contribution as psychoanalysts, in an arena that is conceptually so crowded and confused, is that of going beyond the phenomenic level and analysing what it is, at conscious and unconscious levels, that leads an individual to commit incest, as well as understanding the damage that incest inflicts on the victim's development process and organization of psychic structure, disarticulating the maturational phases of the Oedipus complex and relative drive vicissitudes.

The limit—but at the same time the resource—of the psychoanalytic approach is the impossibility of tracing clear boundaries between active and passive, between victim and perpetrator, seduced and seducer. Certainly, there are essential and unrenounceable differences on the moral plane of responsibility and of guilt, but in clinical reality these become organized into an ambiguous psychopathological interweaving of specularity, projective and introjective identifications, and the compulsion to repeat.

Psychoanalysis has always been concerned with the study of unconscious fantasies and the anxieties that lead to renunciation and the inhibition of incestuous drives, as a constant drama of the Oedipus complex and of growth. More rarely, it has to confront the incestuous acting out through failure of the maturational process and of the inhibitory mechanisms. Starting from the clinical experience of all of us and from knowledge accumulated in over a century of psychoanalysis, it is the fascinating task of this meeting to investigate how these two poles of the problem, with all their interpersonal and intrapsychic articulations, have or have not changed during the course of time together with the changes in the type of society and family in which we and our patients are living.

Beginning with these premises, I think that two important advances in post-Freudian psychoanalysis today allow us to make a critical review of the theme of incest:

- the exploration of the very early, so-called pre-oedipal levels of psychism;
- knowledge about the feminine aspect of women, acquired mainly—but not only—by woman psychoanalysts.

The pre-oedipal levels

Classically, the theme of incest has been dealt with in the oedipal dimension as being a "nuclear complex of neurosis" that arises as a desire and wish on the part of the little boy or girl within the "triangular" problems of the primary scene. Real incest, regardless of the stage of life at which it occurs, brings these early fantasies to the forefront (in both protagonists, although each one according to his/her dimension and history). But it also has the disruptive effect (mainly in the victim) of disorganizing the coordinates of development that should have been guaranteed by the overcoming of the Oedipus complex; in particular, the two basic differences between "big" and "little" and between "male" and "female".

However, as we know, since the 1940s psychoanalysis has dedicated much attention to the very early phases of development—the so-called pre-oedipal levels—and to the pathologies deriving from the deficit and relational distortions taking place during these stages of life. (This has sometimes rather overshadowed, both in theory and in clinical practice, the analysis of the oedipal levels and relative conflicts.) It is necessary, on the other hand, to understand how much the very early history of an individual counts in respect to the way in which he/she arrives at the oedipal appointment; especially regarding the way he/she may act—or react—to the incestuous impact. Indeed, as I try to show later, in the case of incest, problems often come into play that are much more archaic than those of Oedipus. Today's greater clinical experience provides us with better opportunities for analysing also from the perspective of the the adult seducer the incestuous thematics and the profound motives for his/her actions.

We must therefore reconsider how the two levels—oedipal and pre-oedipal—may intertwine with each other; with what internal endowment the individual arrives at the oedipal crossroads; how the previous evolutionary vicissitudes developed beginning with the undifferentiated sensuality of primary auto-eroticism, from the separation–individuation processes to the primary identification–disidentification processes; how the first defensive organizations against archaic anxieties of integration–non-integration, loss of self and annihilation, were articulated. In other words, we must try to explore to what extent the successive stages of growth were conditioned by what happened before; but also, retroactively, how much the "after" reorganizes and reconstitutes the sense of the "before".

The way in which these questions are formulated and confronted inevitably depends on how we conceptualize the very early levels. Thus, we come up against the thorniest problem of present-day psychoanalysis—the confrontation/competition between models—that produces endless and, I am afraid, insoluble diatribes.

The different models

Here, I attempt to roughly outline the characteristic differences between the conceptualization of the very early levels and their role within the various schools of psychoanalysis, using (with gratitude, although summarily) Pine's scheme of the so-called "four psychologies" (1999).

"Drive psychology"

Some analysts, rigorously faithful to Freud's drive model, do not seem to have problems because they do not give much relevance to post-Freudian thought, and therefore not even to pre-oedipal levels. The individual is seen essentially in terms of drives and their vicissitudes of struggle to satisfy needs, and of unconscious fantasies that produce conflict, guilt, and anxiety.

"Ego psychology"

Ego psychologists see development as a fairly linear process; as the capacity for progressive adaptation between internal world and external world, within a dialectic between reality testing and defences, according to which evolutionary failures become translated into ego defects. Also psychopathologic constellations can reflect forms of primary attachment, the source of an albeit distorted "feeling of security", independently of what it may cost in suffering or deficit.

"Self-psychology"

In contrast, self-psychologists, who explore the emerging subjective states, the delimitation of the boundaries between self and not-self, and the degrees of differentiation, have attached great importance to problems and pathologies connected with the "dual", the "maternal" and the "pregenital". The hypothesis is that there exists a stage in which there is not yet any discrimination between self and the other, between first and second object, and that development proceeds through the construction of psycho–physical boundaries and identity nuclei. In this context, some analysts believe that the "pre-oedipal" is also "pre-conflictual"; that is to say, at the origin the drives have not yet come into play, or at least they do not yet have any mental sense. This results in a model that presupposes a specific dual/pregenital/pre-oedipal and—earlier still—narcissistic space, with specific problems and specific times of elaboration in psychoanalytic cure.

"Object relations psychology"

These analysts have taken the Oedipus complex back to a very early phase, the so-called "very early Oedipus". They postulate a miniature, vaguely sketched triangularity right from the archaic phase of life. Thus, in the mother there is already the father, even though in a pseudo-triangulation, immersed in the heart of psychotic anxieties and under the predominance of orality, with continuous fluctuation between object relation and identification, between partial and total objects, and between schizo–paranoid anxieties and depressive anxieties. Breast and penis are thus equivalent and, to a certain extent, also mother and father, so that from the Freudian theory of "sole genital" we are said to have passed to that of "sole parent". In this picture, temporality has less value because "in the transversal section" everything is already always there, in absolute contemporaneity. (Szpilka, 1985, calls it "archaeological model".) Each trauma in infancy is thus believed to be preserved internally as a trace that is continually put back into the scene. New events are assimilated to the old dramas according to the dimension of primary anxieties.

I should like to say that, personally, I find it difficult to definitely side with one model or another. I recognize the merits and the limits of all of them. Perhaps, like many of us, I find myself using, at the preconscious level, various "implicit" theories (Sandler, 1983), even though they may be incompatible with each other. I would not like our discussion to become a confrontation between models, but rather that we should together look at the complexity of the matter, the technical impact of our choices and the clinical challenges deriving therefrom, particularly regarding the problem of incest. For example, by carrying to extremes the presuppositions of self-psychology, one can say that an adult patient "has not yet reached the level of ambivalence" and that "Oedipus is still to come", leading to technical consequences that are anything but banal. Thus, there would be no point in providing interpretations of transference or of aggressiveness as long as one is moving in this area, leading to the paradox of believing that one should not interpret the oedipal level until the pre-oedipal level has been analysed.

However, not even an approach according to the fourth model, that takes into careful account the primitive vicissitudes of aggressiveness in the projections/reintrojections play but according to the concept of "very early Oedipus", would allow us to deal with the qualitative difference that is produced if the Oedipus "complex" is understood as being a new and quantitatively different event that, thanks to the retroactive effect, sets in motion the symbolic reorganization of intrapsychic structure and interpersonal relations. In my view, it would not be possible in this way to account for the havoc determined by incest precisely in the oedipal crossroads, which can be considered as a new and transformational structurizing moment and regulator of the super-ego coodinates and of its discriminatory function between good and bad, thus of introjection of the rule, and its function of protection as well as the administration of guilt.

An opportunity to focus on the possible theoretic and clinical divergences is offered to us by some acute observations by Mitchell

(1997), who realized that in certain cases of paedophilia and of incest by male adults on their children of both sexes, it was not a real sexual drive that came into play, but a primitive problem of envious attack against the female wife/mother who looked after these children instead of looking after the male adults. A very archaic pathology, therefore, within the realm of the pre-oedipal or, if you wish, of the very early Oedipus. I think that, in fact, this interpretation on the primitive levels of envy throws a new light on incest and paedophilia; but I also think that the oedipal levels involved are in any case not indifferent (for example, they turn towards sexualization an aggressiveness that could have expressed itself through explicit beatings).

Even though we may admit that in the clinical reality of the same person there can be all this—and even more—it is quite different to consider the problems that cause and are caused by incest (and then to interpret them) according to castration anxieties or primary anxieties of attack/penetration/reprisal, or else according to the need of contact, the anxiety of annihilation, and of loss of self. As Amati Mehler (1992) observes in "Love and male impotence", in the adult age the mature capacity to love and to fully live sexuality requires that each individual is able to host inside themselves the whole range of emotions and passions, and can recognize in themselves and then share with the other both the primitive fusional levels implying the momentary loss of boundaries, as well as those more mature drive levels of recognition of otherness, of sexuality, and of that quota of healthy aggressiveness that the complete love relationship requires. But it is precisely the availability of a man—and of a woman, I may add—to immerse him/herself and re-emerge from the love relationship without too much fear, that depends not only on how the oedipal drama has been resolved, but also on how, in its time, the process of differentiation between self and object unfolded.

She writes:

> . . . It is precisely the intricate separation and individuation processes, within the complex interweaving of regressive symbiotic trends, as opposed to differentiation—with its necessary quotas of aggressive drives in the service of growth—that may fall short of a sufficiently adequate outcome in terms of permeable self-object boundaries.. [Amati Mehler, 1992, p. 477]

That is to say, mature love means knowing how to share with the same person both the passion, when the object is at the same time the target of libidinous and aggressive drives, as well as the more archaic sensual pregenital affects, until reaching the "oceanic" totalizing experience of fusion[7] that entails the temporary annulment of boundaries without the fear of not re-emerging. This is exactly what has failed in the person who seeks an incestuous experience. For whoever commits incest is unable to share joint intimacy, because the capacity to recognize the other as such is lacking, as is the capacity to identify with him/her as being different. The "true" other— whatever the "soft" or violent form that the incest takes—cannot be met because, previously, the process of pre-oedipal differentiation has been too weak and precarious. In the majority of cases, the inequality between the two members of the incestuous couple is immense, in an emotional relationship that is tyrannical and parasitic. There remains to be understood, from one case to another obviously, the qualitative and quantitative entity of this imbalance, such as in incest between siblings, for example; these are situations of lesser abuse than occurs between adults and children, between parents and sons/daughters, but on the clinical plane, they are the generators of just as much damage and confusion.

The problem of the interweaving between oedipal and pre-oedipal levels is illustrated in more detail in the following brief clinical vignette.[8]

> Y, a 22-year-old male patient, tells the analyst that during his childhood he was for a long time "visited" by his father in his bedroom. The man would get up from the bed that he shared with his wife, go into the bathroom to urinate and then, with his penis still dripping, would creep into his son's bed and rub himself against him. In the meantime, the mother would continue sleeping, apparently unawares. For the rest of the time, their family life continued normally.

As an abstract conceptual exercise, let us try to formulate a list of hypotheses on the psychopathological motivations of the father according to the possible different conceptual frameworks.

- One could think of the man's need for tenderness and of physical contact, as he searches for a warm and dry welcome in the body of the child.

- Or one could emphasize the man's omnipotent fantasy that his penis dripping with urine is a powerful phallus, the bearer of fertility.
- Or again, in symbolic equivalence, that it is a breast offering nourishment.
- If, on the other hand, we tune in to the more mature levels relative to the elaboration of Oedipus, we could think of his search for sexual pleasure—the homosexual aspects—in order to avoid castration anxiety.
- Taking for granted that everything is plausible and potentially co-existent, one could also—and with good reason—think of a play of projection of infantile parts of himself in the son, thus satisfying his old incestuous wishes regarding his own father.

From time to time, therefore, one can choose to emphasize the need, or the sexual or aggressive drive in its various forms (from destructive narcissistic attack to envious attack directed towards a partial or total object, or a part of the self projected on to or confused with the other). The essential point, and I think the most difficult, is not to anchor our thought (and the patient) to a sole level of development; but to try to consider how even the most archaic functioning and defensive mechanisms have, in any case, passed through the oedipal crossroads, deforming it and being transformed by it. For example, using the same clinical vignette, in the background can be seen the deficit of archaic vicissitudes of the man with his mother, the confusion between male and female; but also the distortion of the oedipal triangle with mother and father that is expressed in reality with the significant exclusion of the woman—the wife/mother who sleeps in the other room—usurping her role, exploiting her complicity, and in any case annulling the two fundamental dictates of Oedipus—recognition of the difference between big and little and between male and female.

The feminine

Let us now consider the feminine contribution to post-Freudian psychoanalysis: the patrimony of knowledge about the development process and feminine identity acquired mainly, but not solely, thanks to the thinking of women psychoanalysts themselves. As we know, the generation of the women pioneers formulated against their own sex the most deprecating and ferocious theories, thereby sanctioning a mutilated identity dominated by the triad of "masochism, passivity, narcissism", condemned to an eternal infancy without instincts, and consigned to a destiny of envy and lack. Today, however, we can count on a rich patrimony of ideas that have reconsidered the identity vicissitudes of women as regards gender and sex, and that have also, of necessity, unhinged and then reconstructed, in the relational dimension, the classical parameters of masculine identity as well.

In the context of our meeting, planned and organized by our colleagues of COWAP with sensibility and attention to the theoretic and clinical problems of the feminine identity, I do not need to discuss such concepts that have by now become firmly established, including the possibility of finding *après coup* in Freud himself precursory intuitions in this sense. (I shall not include a review of the literature on the matter because, fortunately, it would be too long; also because it deals with matters that are well known to all of us. I refer the reader to previous works listed in my final bibliography and to the relative biographies quoted therein.)

Women are by now recognized as protagonists and are thus responsible for the whole range of sexual and aggressive drives, whether in a horizontal direction towards men or in a vertical direction in the parent–child relationship. Regarding the theme of incest, therefore, there is a radical change in the prospect of "strong attachment" of the little girl to the mother during the first years of infancy, mentioned by Freud (1931b); and an even greater change in the sense of the subsequent brusque detachment, loaded with hostility and resentment, that was once attributed to penis envy and that would be the cause of the "veering" towards the father. From Melanie Klein onwards, the woman's wish for a child will no longer automatically be seen as a narcissistic device to compensate for the lack of a penis, but as an object in itself of drive investment, whether healthy or pathological. In contrast, in as much as every human being, both male or female and with dramatic equality, is at the same time the bearer of a deficiency and of an excess (De Simone, 2002), there is more evidence today of the regressive pathological quality of cases in which certain women who are unable to tolerate an intimate sense of void and incompleteness, stubbornly insist on becoming pregnant at any cost as the "solution" for a narcissistic flaw. Dinora Pines (1992), for example, understands very well that there must be a differentiation between a woman's wish to become pregnant and her wish to have a child; and how the experience of maternity can sometimes promote maturation and reinforcement of feminine identity, while at other times it can regressively push the woman back to primary identification with the mother, in a trap of early ambivalence.

Nor is it less important to consider how the bodily experience of pregnancy and the birth of a child can sometimes bring about a real upheaval in a woman's sexuality and the relationship with her partner. For example, quite frequently after the birth of a child, the couple may have difficulties in their sex life. In the past this was thought to be only the man's problem because he was insufficiently attracted by the woman's transformed body. At most, it was recognized that there is a generic sexual unavailability on the part of the woman, who is too concentrated on her child. Instead, for both of them a profound equivalence is in force according to which becoming a mother means becoming the mother, and the refusal of sexuality is the consequence of the fear of fantasies of incest between mother and child.

We may recall the old saying (mentioned also by Lévi-Strauss) according to which habit and routine weaken desire. This would be a normal, "natural" and therefore so-called biological and not analysable phenomenon: not a repressed desire, but a flame that is extinguished. Freud's reflections in 1910h seem to be somewhat more convincing; he describes two "currents" in the psychosexual development of the human being: one is tender and affectionate, the other sensual and sexual. With maturity, the two currents can be integrated within the self and then directed towards the same woman: but often, defensively, they are split and distributed on to two different women—to the wife/mother goes the affection, and to the lover goes the passion. The cause of the splitting, therefore, is incestuous fantasy; were it not for the fact that, today, we find in the woman as well the "typical" male splitting of the past.

I can present several clinical examples to illustrate this, such as that of a woman patient of mine who no longer wanted to make love with her partner whenever the relationship was stabilized in a situation of living together and making plans for the future. She made up for this coldness by having sporadic affairs with occasional partners.

Now that the sexuality of women is no longer denied, we can clearly see in them, too, the deficits and the neurotic solutions. Another delicate terrain is that of breast-feeding (regarding which I have been able to acquire considerable analytic experience).[9] The sensations aroused when a baby sucks the breast can, in fact, be the cause of complicated emotional upheavals in the mother. Some women are frightened by the pleasure that this experience produces in them; they have difficulty in distinguishing pleasure from pain, and they react with anxiety and by refusing the baby. Others, on the other hand, are equally frightened by the irruption of drive quotas of excitation in the relationship with the baby, but they find a way out by cutting away a part of themselves; i.e. they react defensively by inhibiting all desire and sexual impulse with the husband.

This reminds me of a young woman patient who, ever since she became a mother, felt uncontrollably "annoyed" if her husband kissed her nipples; the sensations aroused in her when she breast-fed were too similar. Therefore, in order to protect the relationship with the baby, sexuality had to be excluded.

We must also consider the different conscious and unconscious attitudes of women according to the sex of their children; how they experience the mixture of pleasure and excitation caused by the sucking at the breast of a boy or of a girl baby. In the past it was often thought that there was an unbalanced "mouth/breast intro-jection" with girl babies, destined to confirm the identity of the mother as nurturer; while to boy babies was assigned the function of "narcissistic compensation" (Argentieri, 1982a). Today, unfortu-nately, the events of maternity do not always produce the perfec-tion and harmony that the conquests of these last decades would lead us to expect. Sometimes, in the guise of "ideology", the girl baby is "preferred" as the mother seeks in her a self-referring narcissistic link. Events such as these are a kind of "litmus paper" for partial solutions of the Oedipus complex. In them, the priority of very early levels over adult levels is outstandingly evident, as well as the weight of unresolved problems of separation–individu-ation and of so-called dis-identification of the woman from the mother. Incestuous fantasies—both heterosexual and homosexual (it is hard to know which are the most disquieting)—with children are interwoven with the anxieties of annihilation and re-engulfment in the primary object.

The problem, therefore, is on the one side to discriminate, and on the other side to integrate within the self and in relationships, the various levels of development and of areas of psychic functioning. That is, to be able to differentiate without splitting. I think that this is what has failed in those who commit incest, and it is inexorably transmitted to those who suffer it: a lack of intrapsychic and interpersonal distinction between the tender, sensorial aspects and the erotic drive aspects.[10]

I also want to refer briefly to the interesting observations of Estela Welldon who, in her work as a forensic psychotherapist, was the first to understand the special difficulty that women have in making themselves heard, in public or private consultations, regarding their fears and anxieties in relation to their incestuous impulses towards their children. Often, operators unconsciously refuse to come into contact with incestuous themes, even more disquieting if they concern the mother. Their personal defence is thus camouflaged as kindly reassurance, and promotes denial; even more so because maternal incestuous acts are performed with less sensational gestures and can be mistaken for intimacy and tenderness.

> This brings to mind the case of a woman patient of mine, V., who during a psychotic and delusional crisis asked to go into a clinic, although continuing to come to daily sessions, because she was afraid of giving in to her incestuous impulses towards her two little girls and of masturbating them. She understood that this sexual impulse was at the service of a deeper desire to re-engulf the children in a regressive fusional dimension; and this was equivalent to the fantasy of herself being re-engulfed by her mother. At home, she complained, there were no men; only nannies, maids, even the dog was female. And so was her analyst . . . By invoking a man, a father, she expressed her need for a presence that was bodily different and would guarantee a differentiating function by collapsing this symbolic function—according to her psychotic thinking—into the concreteness of a male-who-was-different.

What my patient was imploring so painfully is sometimes enacted clandestinely by mothers who sexualize the relationship in order to maintain indefinite possession of their children. They confer on their sons a premature and undeserved "oedipal victory", thus depriving them of the structuring act of confrontation with the father who, in his turn, is probably quite happy to avoid the challenge, leaving his son "in hostage" to the mother.

Protection and guilt

As we know, a complicated and contorted structure of guilt grows up around incest; ubiquitous in the case of unconscious fantasies, very unevenly distributed in the case of actual incest. Paradoxically, it is rare for the seducer to be oppressed with feelings of guilt; indeed, the act itself, with its relative defences, has the aim of avoiding it (Speziale Bagliacca, 1997). In the rare cases when I have met someone in therapy who had committed incest, the idea that his behaviour could be harmful for the person who had suffered it was intolerable for him. Admitting that his body, his "love", the pleasure deriving from it, could be damaging unleashed the most violent resistances, both as avoidance of guilt and as narcissistic insult. The victim, on the other hand, is almost always tormented by a sense of guilt, with mixed feelings of resentment, shame, worthlessness, loss of self-esteem. This is the symptom of the damage to the structure that the incestuous experience has provoked in the intrapsychic relationships between id, ego, and superego. The superego, with its normative, punitive, and protective functions is, in fact, one of the "outcomes" of the superceding of the oedipal knot, and among its connotations is the sign of how these events have been solved.

As Szpilka (1985) summarized in the previously mentioned work, according to ancient Hegelian philosophy the value of the Oedipus complex as a reorganizing moment of psychism consists in the fact that the "good" and the "bad", until then simply in opposition to each other according to the dimension of the pleasure–unpleasure principle, now enter into a more complex dialectical relationship. "Goodness" and "good" no longer coincide; nor do "evil" and "bad". What is good on one level—enjoyment of the mother's body—after the oedipal awareness becomes bad, as it is forbidden and the source of guilt and anguished expectations of castration.

On the contrary, by renouncing what could be pleasurable but is the cause of unpleasure, the approval is earned of the superego as a superior gain. ". . . love and hate enter into a dialectic complexity, where the good and the bad cease being absolute categories, self-administered on simple biological grounds . . ." (pp. 42–43).

A paradoxical but rigorous interweaving is produced; a symbolic network of complex legitimacies from which all human "values" derive—cognitive, ethical, and aesthetic—as well as the basic feelings of interior calmness and self-esteem. This is one of the gate-posts that becomes unhinged in incest, where the goodness and the evil, the good and the bad—and therefore the feeling of guilt—remain in an area of confusion, similar to that of perverse organizations.

A patient, C who, when he became adult, was given to risky and disordered sexual activities, was very difficult to handle in the analytic relationship. He assumed an attitude of scornful superiority towards me, treating my interpretations concerning the damage he was doing to himself and others as if they were the timid worries of a moralistic little prude. He managed to protect himself from anxiety and guilt through the massive use of splitting and denial that, after a long time, began to show some cracks—at least in his dreams, such as the time he dreamt that his penis "was therapeutic", but then he saw that its tip was covered in pus and a piece of gauze; or else that there was "something" spherical and gray in his brain: a precious and very rare pearl . . . or perhaps was it a bullet? . . . But the most indicative dream is the one in which he recalls: "All my gums were swollen and sore, I was anxiously showing them to my ex-parents-in-law. I was asking them how to cure myself. I entrusted myself to them completely . . . to those traitors! . . . Those rotters who did me so much harm! . . . and I was so sure they liked me!" (He suffered very much when his in-laws turned against him during his separation from his wife and children.) He associated that his gums really were bleeding and that this increased his worries about contracting HIV. In the manifest transferential dimension, I was able to show him how he continuously risked directing his needs, impulses, and desires towards unreliable people (for example when he looked for "affection" in his nocturnal sexual meanderings with strangers, or in the financial swindles in which he repeatedly became involved while searching for the miraculous deal); and, as a result, how much all this was expressed in his unreliability regarding his present wife and his children.

In order for the passage from dual linearity to the oedipal triangularity to take place, it is necessary to have on stage the desiring subject, the desired object and a "third" who prohibits. Thus, for the oedipal knot to organize itself and produce "structure", whether normal or pathological, the individual must be immersed in a "culturalized" world, that provides an external prohibiter that can then be interiorized as internal legislator. In fact, Freud wrote (1913–1914) that ". . . the beginnings of religion, morals, society and art converge in the Oedipus complex . . . on the basis of one single concrete point—man's relation to his father" (pp. 156–157). The sad point is that the one who commits the incest is often the father, thus causing the maximum of confusion and disorder.

But how much of the introjection process of the superego functions depends on the relationship with the real father? In psychoanalysis, especially according to certain models, much emphasis is put on the figure of the Father (with a capital F) as the carrier of "logos" and of law, as he who promotes conflict and growth. Yet, in my opinion, not enough attention is paid to the distinction between the father and the symbolic paternal function, between penis and phallus. The superego, in fact, derives from parental introjections, that are as much maternal as they are paternal.

As Sigmund Freud (1923b) writes in a fundamental "note" in "The ego and the id", too often neglected also by psychoanalysts, we must not forget that when we analyse early infancy we are usually speaking about the relationship with the mother. ". . . Perhaps it would be safer to say 'with the parents'; for before a child has arrived at definite knowledge of the difference between the sexes . . . it does not distinguish in value between its father and its mother" (ibid., p. 31, footnote 1). Similarly, according to the structural value of the primary scene process and of the Oedipus complex, the advent of the "second object" does not mean that the father appears on the scene for the first time; but that he is no longer experienced as being homologous, equivalent to the "first object" that, in its turn, is not only the real mother. The vicissitudes of separation foresee the physical detachment, and the intrapsychic discrimination between self and not-self, as well as the distinction between the various objects. The promotion of this process is the task of the mother as well as of the father. It is the adult parental function of the institution of the "law"; it is a developmental goal that is perpetually renegotiated, not an automatic "stopping point" provided by the official sex of the parent. In this sense, incest with the father or with the mother takes the form of homo- or hetero-sexual not only according to the sex of the son/daughter, but also according to the more or less developed relational levels that are put into play.[11] Likewise, the protective function is as much mater-nal as paternal, as long as they are both able to unite gentleness with the capacity to hold and firmly contain: a "taking care of", a psycho-physical *holding* in the Winnicottian sense, in which there is no irruption of levels of drive excitation.

> Unfortunately this is not what happened to A, today a young woman, wife, and mother, who, from the beginning of adolescence, was for many years subjected to the overpowering sexuality of her father, surrounded by the indifference of her older siblings and the helpless resentment of her mother. Sometimes at night she would lock herself in her room, while her parents argued. Her father would sarcastically say to her, ridiculing her frail, pathetic self-defence, "Do you think a locked door is enough to stop me?" Every now and then her mother would submit her to painful questioning, accusing her of deceit and lying; she even reached the point, when the girl was older, of insulting her on the street, shouting "Whore!" She blamed her, but she did not protect her.
>
> In analysis A once told of a heart-rending childhood memory. When she was ten or twelve years old she was in bed and pretending to be asleep. Someone came into her room and caressed her on the cheek. She felt a tormented feeling of great emotion and did not want to open her eyes. Who was it who caressed her? How she wished it could have been her father . . .
>
> I think that the desperate need of this patient to be able to evoke within herself a protective function, not confused with sexuality, cannot be expressed any better; a "nostalgia" for something that has never been, and that she calls "father".[12]

I take this opportunity to add that occasionally—in spite of dramatic stories of repeated and very early traumatic incest such as this one—the victims have extraordinary individual resources of vitality that allow them to redeem their own destiny. This is what is happening to A, who has managed to form her own family and also to enjoy sexuality. In my own clinical experience, it frequently happens that both male and female patients evoke such a nostalgic image—the more yearned for and missed, the less it was really enjoyed; it must be strong and protective, but also tender and good, without conflicts, contrasts, aggressiveness. It takes the name and the appearance of the father, but it is a clandestine version, idealized and split, that we may call "maternal father" (Argentieri, 1999).

Father and paternal function

It is difficult but necessary not to diminish the specific importance of the father, keeping clearly in mind the two coordinates of the interpersonal and the intrapsychic dimension of his real person and of his (but not only his) symbolic function transmissible from generation to generation. How much do the social and cultural mutations relative to the father, to his presence and to his role in present-day families, count in the organization of the Oedipus complex nowadays? For about half a century, since the sociologist Mitscherlich entitled his best known work *Towards a Society Without a Father* (1963), the rhetorical absence of the paternal figure dominates in Western culture. Indeed, the general decline of the so-called "principle of authority" could not but overwhelm, for better or for worse, also the image of the Father and his symbolic value as superior power. For example, in clinical notes about a patient's family history, we often find the words "absence of the father", following a stereotype that nowadays no longer requires specifications as to what extent this absence is material or affective.

On a more commonplace everyday basis, complaints about the scarce significance of men during the whole period of time from birth to the growing-up of children have been a constant theme of feminist battles, and it was subsequently with dismay that we saw the passage—almost with no solution of continuity—from the authoritarian father to the father who is not there at all (Pazzagli, 1999). Therefore, while the authoritarian father of the past has left the stage, new types of absences are appearing. As a result of separations and divorces, there is an increase of emarginated fathers or, in any case, of marginal fathers; sometimes embittered and suffering, sometimes collusively fugitive, reduced to the role of "visiting father", every other Sunday plus holidays. It seems to me that the widespread complaint about the so-called "loss of values" in present-day society is also closely linked to this theme.

How could all this not affect the way in which the Oedipus complex is articulated and manifested? I am thinking, for example, about what kind of relationship an adolescent girl can establish with a father who has lived separated from her for years. In the past, the father was the appointed guardian of his daughter's sexual repression (the socially accepted other side of the incestuous father). But nowadays, the oedipal play has been completely upset. The function of the authority that prohibits is unacceptable, while the need to re-conquer a bit of oedipal intimacy risks slipping into the "confusion of languages". The most frequent "solution" is that of avoiding the conflict through tenderness. Thus, in order to escape the anxieties of intimacy with a father who is a stranger and absent in everyday life, the Oedipus complex is often acted out "outside", in reality, by sexual and love affairs with older men and for periods of time that are considerably longer than the physiological period.

The mutation of the defences

The basic paradigms of psychism do not change with the changing of customs, and one or two generations are certainly not sufficient to transform the foundations of our theory. I think that in psychoanalysis the Oedipus complex, even though by now most of us write it with a small "o", has preserved its main evolutionary, affective, and cognitive meaning under the shield of drives. What might have changed, if anything, are the defences. We cannot disregard the fact that we are immersed in a reality that, in our advanced Western society, changes rapidly: single-parent families, precarious and atypical recompositions of family nuclei, technological procreations, maternal fathers, men and women turning towards homosexuality in advanced age, homosexuality itself that has changed its psychological and psychopathological features.

Today our tolerance of atypical expressions of sexuality is greater: the cross-dressing of adults and children, virtual sexuality, virtual paedophilia, sex tourism, the category of transgender, that now unites transvestites and trans-sexuals in a single category.

Even perversions have now slipped from specific syndrome to generic symptom, from a sexual register to that of a regressive auto-sensorial modality. At the same time, there has been a general slackening in adult parental functions, with difficulty in imposing rules and limits. As we have all been able to see, for at least two generations this has produced—for better or for worse—personality structures that are less rigid, more flexible, and with a superego that is less imposing and an ego that is more fragile. I am also struck by the "endogamic" style of many groups of young people, where couples are formed and break up always within a closed circuit of reassuring familiarity. After the separations (so to speak) they continue seeing each other and being friends; even unfaithfulness occurs without conflict or passion. It seems as though the illusion of being able to find everything within the tight circuit of the *heim-lich* is extended to the whole group.[13] And thus the oedipal knot is loosened, if not avoided. The "differences" between big and small, male and female, gender identity, maturity, individuation—once again, for better or for worse—besides being "feeble" are no longer an absolute value.

The "classical" resolution of the Oedipus complex entails that, in order to avoid castration anxiety, the oedipal rivalry has to be renounced. But who can we rival today? Where are the fathers to challenge? In "Totem and taboo" Freud (1913–1914) wrote: ". . . they are afraid precisely because they would like to, and the fear is stronger than the desire . . ." (p. 31) But, who strikes fear today? The paradox is that the fear has weakened, but so has the desire. We often prefer to find a regressive refuge in the niche of undifferentiation, well before having to confront castration anxiety or, in any case, the incompleteness of each individual.

For both males and females the acquisition of identity was considered to be inseparable from the acceptance of the prohibition of incestuous desires. In the past, many authoritative authors, from Grünberger (1977) to Fornari (1982), asserted that the Oedipus complex fades when the oedipal desire is perceived as impossible.[14] The prize is in taking a distance from confusion. But what if, instead, the confusion has organized itself as a defence? As many have observed, the pathologies of our patients change, and today's defence mechanisms are not so much in the dimension of repression or of repressive attitudes. With increasing frequency we find ourselves having to contend with splitting and denial; and even more so, at the ambiguous boundary with so-called normality, with primitive defence organizations of non-integration and ambiguity. That is to say, the persistence of the pre-oedipal defences heavily mortgages the Oedipus complex.[15]

In a context such as this, of a general regressive defensive tendency towards indifference and undifferentiated, can it be that even incest gives rise to less anxiety, less guilt, less horror?

A young father, suffering and resentful because of sexual abstinence, turned out by his wife, who had firmly ensconced herself in their marriage bed with the new-born baby, had to sleep with his son in a double sofa-bed. He tells me that during the night, when half-asleep, he realized he had an erection and that his penis was resting against the child's body. What is most significant is that he tells me this as if it were something trivial, in an apathetic tone and completely devoid of any disquieting feelings.

Also at the conceptual level, even in the psychotherapeutic field we tend today to use the more generic term of "abuse". Finally, on the social level, the proposed law to de-penalize incest between consenting adults that was presented—not without scandal—in a progressive Sweden in 1978, is today reproposed in England without too much public outcry.

Does this mean that the cultural and psychological barrier against incest is crumbling? Can we consider that the classical emphasis on the damage caused by incest, that disrupts the sense of the two great differences, the metabolisms of anxiety and guilt and of the correlated thought processes, is now to be considered outdated? In spite of all this, I think that incest produces damage just as it did in the past and perhaps even more so, but more subtly, because destructiveness is manifested in forms that are covert, ambiguous, and discreet. It penetrates into a psychological terrain that is already devastated, in a state of crisis, where the "confusion of languages" is in action, and where individuals remain in an eternal "mirror phase" in a combination of co-responsibilities, unhappiness, and bad faith. The more developed oedipal drive levels are always involved in the problem of incest; but with increasing frequency they can go to the service of other levels, and of the regressive needs for contact and the annulment of boundaries.

The most illustrious victim is the thought process. In Bionian terms (1961), the impact of the cognitive interrogative on one's origins and one's own identity becomes fragmented and weakened.

Referring to Sophocles' *Oedipus Rex*, John Steiner (1993) says that the fulcrum of the tragedy is not the search for the truth, but the inability to conceal it from oneself in spite of the desperate attempt to keep it hidden. But today even the concept of truth itself appears to be blurred and enveloped in the complacent veil of ambiguity.

As psychoanalysts, we too are presented with hitherto unknown problems relating to incest, and with new challenges at the countertransferential level. From the father we have turned to the mother, and from the sexual drive to the aggressive drive in its archaic manifestations of non-recognition of alterity. Consequently, the modalities of the transference are no longer in the dimension of the classical erotic trap; but they take on more viscous and elusive forms that are responsible for paralysing that healthy quota of aggressiveness that promotes maturation and growth. It seems as though, with the passing of time and history, human destiny does not change; forced from one generation to the other to confront the eternal problem of incest, it wavers between fascination and horror in a conflict that seems to coincide with the equally eternal antinomy between Eros and Thanatos, and between the drives of life and of death—an antinomy that, as we all know, in its most subtle forms assumes the beguiling vestiges of regressive attraction.

Notes

1. Translated from Italian by Jill Cucco.
2. For a review of the theories on the prohibition of incest, I have used, and recommend a reading of, the bibliography quoted by F. Ceccarelli (*Il tabù dell'incesto*, Turin, Einaudi, 1978).
3. For many years I have worked with G. Dal Pozzo of "Telefono Rosa", a telephonic help line for women with problems.
4. It is in this realm that Joseph Sandler (Sandler & Fonagy, 1997) has built a bridge between psychoanalysis and the neurosciences, regarding the possibility of discriminating, in the adult patient, the memories of a seduction really experienced in infancy from one that was merely fantasised.

5. I refer the reader to the articles by M. Mancia (1985) and S. Argentieri (1983) about the pseudo-scandal orchestrated by A. Masson on this subject.

6. I refer to the book by the Japanese psychoanalyst Takeo Doi (1971) translated into Italian twenty years later entitled *Anatomia della dipendenza*. *"Amae"* could be defined as the absolute loving indulgence that exists in the fusional state.

7. I refer to the Preface that in 1954 Emilio Servadio wrote to Freud's paper "Inhibition, symptom and anxiety".

8. I thank my colleague, Geni Valle, for allowing me to quote this excerpt from her clinical case (in the course of publication) which, evidently, she analysed from the perspective of the son.

9. For a long time I have worked together with Laura Pennisi of the Centro Nascita Montessori (Montessori Birth Centre).

10. I refer to the thought of Eugenio Gaddini who, following Winnicott, distinguishes right from the very early mental processes a "psycho-sensorial" area of contact within the dimension of imitation, and a "psycho-oral" area within the drives dimension.

11. The distinction between mother and father, male and female, is a long and tortuous process. Both the boy and the girl child have to learn, first of all, to establish the boundaries between self and not-self in the dual dimension; and then to recognize their parents not only as "separate", but also as "different", not the same as each other, within the triadic dimension. In everyday reality, the father can be present since birth, but the baby will not immediately be able to recognize him as such on the intrapsychic and symbolic plane. Only in a second phase will he recognize him in his masculine individuality within the triangular dimension of relationship. We know how much this process, never entirely concluded, is complicated by traps, compromises, arrests, and defences. In the identifications/dis-identification interplay each person constructs their own gender identity and that of the other as a dynamic network of relations rather than a rigid structure. In my view, the male or female identity of each of us is the result of the more or less happy and harmonious integration of various levels: anatomic, biologic, metaphoric, psychological sense of belonging, culturally determined social roles, sexual drives and behaviour.

Too often during the course of development, instead of genuine differentiation, defensive splittings or pseudo-distinctions of partial aspects of the self and of the other can be organized, followed by more or less stable but fictitious recompositions that, at the conscious level, regard the mother and the father, the female sex and the male sex; but at the unconscious level respond to defensive operations against anxieties and conflicts even though at the price of distorting awareness. Thus, for example, the sexual and aggressive drive aspects can be split off and projected on to the father and then on to all males; while the tender, fusional aspects of the relationship remain defensively on the mother, or vice versa. The splittings can be formed not only according to the "classical" horizontal line between "good" and "bad" (penis or breast, alternatively), but also according to the vertical, primitive, or more evolved levels of psychism and the relationship: oedipal and pre-oedipal, tender and eroticized, emotive and intellectual, etc. These cunning and tortuous splittings often persist into the adult age in the form of "theories" on the male and female nature. Obviously, the combinations vary, not only according to the basic fact of whether the subject is born a girl or a boy, but also according to the very early relational vicissitudes and the real characteristics of the parents.

The clinically significant point is that in adult life, in the relationship between a couple, a partner of necessity "inherits" both the fantasies that each one has constructed on the opposite sex, as well as, at deeper levels, those of the primary relationship with the mother. Often, for example, for both the members of the couple, the partner represents the other partner's mother and becomes charged with the relative expectations and possible unresolved conflicts.

12. For this clinical vignette I am indebted to Dr Antonella Gentile, who, under my supervision, is following this very difficult case with great care and intelligence.

13. I think that the theme of "endogamy" has a particular meaning in the psychoanalytic community where, especially at the beginning, there were so many "incestuous" analyses (Argentieri, 1993): fathers with daughters, husbands with wives, blood relations of various degrees taking it in turns on the same couch. Even in modern times there is the much-debated and unresolved question of love affairs between candidates who share the same analyst, or else of "crossed" supervisions and analyses between husband and wife who are both teaching analysts in the same society. As De Lauro Poletti (1990) observed, the monolithic union, even though intrapsychic, in psychoanalytic groups responds to the need to reinforce the bonds of cast as a defence against separation–individuation anxiety. And then there is the immense chapter of real and actual sexual acting out taking place in analysis, with all the complex analogic implications with the problem of incest—a theme that I cannot adequately deal with on this occasion.

14. In *Disordine e dolore precoce,* Thomas Mann gives what I think is the best example of the painful moment in which it is the father who renounces the oedipal privilege when he understands that it can no longer be him who fulfils the wishes and the need for happiness of his little five-year-old daughter

15. I refer to E. Gaddini's concept of "non-integration as defence" and to that of "ambiguity" as described by Bleger.

CHAPTER TWO

Incest(s) and the negation of otherness

Juan Eduardo Tesone

S ome papers condense knowledge of a problem in such an unconditional and impenetrable way that they leave no room for other ideas. The quality of Simona Argentieri's text (in the preceding chapter) lies, I would say, not only in its intertextual polysemy, but also and above all in its interstices. In a very open way, it allows several theories to circulate, suggests rather than concludes, and in this sense is extremely creative, evoking new reflections and encouraging us to use our capacity for reverie. Argentieri has managed to impart an aesthetic dimension to a text that none the less deals with an abject and ignominious theme. This is not because she embellishes it with arabesques, but because she turns a problem that is unspeakable and rarely thought about into something that can be expressed in words, thereby making it think-able, and she gives clinical status to a problem that psychoanalytic theory hardly ever deals with. Psychoanalysts speak a great deal about the Oedipus complex and the prohibition of incest, but rarely of incest that has actually been carried out, perhaps echoing the paradoxical silence forced upon the child victim. In this sense, this symposium is highly relevant, given that it discusses issues about which, until recently, very little has been said, as if the foundations of psychoanalytic theory and the status of fantasy could be found wanting in the face of clinical work with real-life events.

From the outset, as if composing the overture to an opera, Simona Argentieri announces the movements to come. Thinking about incest requires, she reminds us, a transdisciplinary approach that goes beyond the boundaries of psychoanalytic theory.

Referring to the universal nature of the prohibition of incest affirmed by Lévi-Strauss (1947), she takes as her focus its relation to the family. Eschewing any reductionist conception, she gives less emphasis to the biological links that, in constant evolution, may take on different modalities, than to the parental symbolic functions that involve gender identity. I would add that the maternal and paternal functions cannot be defined in isolation; they have to be seen in terms of a dialectic: the maternal function cannot be properly understood except through fantasy and symbolic interaction with the paternal function, and vice-versa. The Oedipus complex, of course, is not simply a prohibition against endogamy; it carries also an authorization that sanctions exogamy. Incest violates this double aspect of the symbolic law by transgressing the prohibition and annulling the urge towards exogamy. Incest as defined by Lévi-Strauss is extended by Françoise Héritier-Augé (1994) to include another type of incest that she calls the "second type" to differentiate it from the Lévi-Strauss model, which is of the first type. She conceives of the prohibition of incest as a problem of circulation of fluids from one body to the other. The basic criterion of incest—according to this anthropological model—is contact between identical humours. This involves what is most fundamental in human society: the construction of the categories of identical and different. If I mention Héritier's theory it is because incest of the Lévi-Strauss type—a beautiful metaphor, in Simona Argentieri's words—does not explain the prohibition in some communities against a man having sexual relations with the sister of his first wife. This second type of incest includes variants such as: a man having sex with each of two sisters, with his wife's daughter (identity of substance between mother and daughter) or symmetrically, a woman having sex with each of two brothers, a woman with her husband's son, etc. The idea is that these same humours are encountered through identical flesh by virtue of the fact that one partner is held in common. The incest takes place through the intermediary of another person. Héritier-Augé's theory proposes a reinterpretation of incest as played out in Sophocles' tragedy: Oedipus, in the act of sexual intercourse with his mother, simultaneously encounters his father, who was in that very place before. One form of incest can conceal another variant, homosexual in nature, which in psychoanalysis has a significant clinical impact. Therefore, it would perhaps be preferable to speak of incests, in the plural, considering the many facets it may take on.

I invite you to follow me in a little imaginary game that, with a touch of humour and not a little despair, reminds us why each member of a family's symbolic structure must occupy only one place, why these places are not interchangeable, and why one person can occupy only one *locus* at any given time.

A psychoanalyst sees a young adult for an initial consultation and asks him what brings him in. The prospective patient replies, "Well, everything started when I married. What a mistake that was! I married a widow with a daughter twenty-five years old who became my stepdaughter. One day, my father visited us and, incredibly enough, fell in love with my stepdaughter. Shortly after, my father and my stepdaughter married. Suddenly, my stepdaughter became my stepmother. Some time later, my wife and I had a son who became my father's brother-in-law, since he is the half-brother of my stepdaughter, who is in turn my father's wife (and therefore my stepmother). Now, my baby is also the half-brother of my stepmother and is therefore a bit my uncle. My wife is also my stepgrandmother because she is the mother of my stepmother. And don't forget that my stepmother is also my stepdaughter. And if we go even further, we see that I am the husband of my stepgrandmother and therefore I am not only my wife's grandson as well as her husband, but also my own grandfather . . . Now you'll understand why I came to see you!"

This fictitious interview helps me to highlight the fact that the family creates and institutes three types of relation:

1.   blood (brother, sister)
2.   marital (wife, husband)
3.   filial (son, daughter).

It is, in this sense, an institution, since it prescribes a certain order. It is clear that the prohibition of incest is not only a prohibition: at the same time as it prohibits, it also makes for order. Each person occupies a defined place, the one assigned to him or her in the family constellation. When incest inverts the order of gender and of generation, the "symbolic network of family relations" is disorganized, as Simona Argentieri emphasizes.

> The psychotic mother of a 16-year-old adolescent, Jérôme, said in her delusion that, in future reincarnations, she could become her son's sister, or her son could be her father, or she could even, with the vicissitudes of successive reincarnations, become her son's wife.

This brief psychotic vignette reveals that the incestuous act is not only physical intercourse; it is at the same time the omnipotent desire to occupy all the *loci* simultaneously: to be father-mother-daughter-son at the same time. The incestuous wish, says Legendre (1985), is a wish to be omnipotent: it desires what is impossible. The prohibition against incest is there to place a limit on this absolute desire. God and the Holy Family—as Legendre points out—know no incest, since God cannot be said to be "lacking" in anything.

The principal function of the family, I insist, is to create otherness. In this sense, it could be argued that motherhood and fatherhood are always, in fact, adoptive, since they require that the other person be acknowledged as such and that the self be part of a chain of transgenerational symbolic functions. Unlike the Oedipus situation, which integrates desire into the law, thereby allowing the emergence of otherness, incest blurs the limits between the members of a family and introduces confusion. Is incest the consequence of an Oedipus complex that is more intense than others? In an earlier paper, I argued—agreeing with Racamier—that incest is in fact quite the opposite. I suggested in that text that the oedipal triangle as such loses its characteristic features and is drawn into a narcissistic problem situation that has much more to do with the family unit as a whole (Tesone, 1994).

The transgression of incest implicitly carries its own denial, to the point that it is trivialized as if it were simply a particular form of family communication. Psychotic foreclosure or perverse disavowal is frequent in this type of family, as in the clinical example of the parental couple discussed by Simona Argentieri, who induced incest between siblings. To my mind, the fact that she uses the word "genitors" and not "parents" is no coincidence, because in this family there were no parents, merely biological genitors. At the very moment the children were induced to commit the incestuous act, they became orphans, as it were—with no one to fulfil the parental role.

The author reminds us that a crucial moment in Freud's work was when he abandoned the theory of seduction-as-a-real-event in favour of the fantasy of seduction, a fantasy which all children share. Argentieri points out that Freud's fundamental clinical intuition was that the fantasy and the real event could have the same pathogenic effect. However, my own clinical experience leads me to believe that the traumatic distress of incest that has been carried out in reality has much a more devastating and deleterious effect on the psyche of a developing self than the organization of an infantile neurosis based on oedipal material that has not been integrated. The sheer weight of the quantitative factor, the ruthless impingement of the drives, bring in their wake even more devastating qualitative damage when the incest has been repeated over time; tantamount to repetitive trauma, it impregnates the psyche with the death drive.

It seems to me a good idea to highlight the radical difference between, on the one hand, the theory of seduction, which provides the very foundations for infantile psychosexuality and repression (which acts as a stimulus for the fantasy representation that leads to the Oedipus complex), and, on the other, the trauma of actual seduction. Laplanche (1986) coined the term "generalized seduction theory", by which he means that the mother is the agent of primary (early) seduction because of her role in taking care of her infant's body; maternal care includes the feeding situation and other intimate contact between her body and that of the infant. This is a necessary seduction, says Laplanche, because it is an integral part of the situation itself. As far as I am concerned, however (Tesone 2001), the traumatic seduction that a child experiences does not fall within that seduction theory. Sexuality operates in such a situation not as a source of life and creator of links, but as a persecutory object that unbinds and has implications of death. The drive of the adult that suddenly bursts through into the child's experience, far from favouring ego integration, leads to what Green (1993) calls "the de-objectifying function of the death drive". The child/

part-object experienced as a pseudopodium of the adult's own ego has no contingent value as a true object for the incestuous genitors; it fulfils a narcissistic need that demands a link between direct descendants.

From that point of view, there is no "soft" form of incest. Even where there is no concomitant physical violence, the mental violence is always present, because the victim's consent does not come into it at all. I agree completely with Simona Argentieri that from the psychoanalytic standpoint it is sometimes difficult to establish the limits between active and passive, abuser and victim, seducer and seduced, since the bond that ties them together is an entangled web of projective and introjective identifications, in which an infinite series of mirror reflections is far too complex to be differentiated. However, I think we need to emphasize that it is precisely this entangled web that the incestuous genitor weaves, using a kind of hypnotic power to immobilize the child in the snares of the abuse. In this sense I would say that incest is always "hard". Children have no chance of making the effect of the incest meaningful as it occurs. They are trapped in the libidinal cartography of the incestuous genitor, subjected to a sexuality that is not totally their own. Later, in the best of cases, they will have to deconstruct this over-abundance of meaning (Tesone 2001) produced by the injection of adult sexuality into the child's developing sexuality; without psychoanalytic treatment, this could leave indelible traces in their libidinal geography.

It is obvious that any psychoanalytic understanding of clinical work with cases of incest will depend on the theoretical perspective from which it is approached, as Simona Argentieri reminds us. With her exceptional capacity for synthesis, she has succeeded in summarizing the main points of the various theories. It is impossible for us to put aside all reference to theory; no clinical eye can look on the material before us without a theoretical backdrop, explicit or implicit, conscious or unconscious. Theory does not prevent something from existing (*ça n'empêche pas d'exister*), as Charcot put it (Freud, 1892–94, p. 139), but it may sometimes hinder communication between colleagues. I suggest that we go along with Simona Argentieri when she proposes that our discussions avoid a clash of theoretical models, so that we can think together about the clinical challenge involved in dealing with the problem of incest. Quoting

Amati Mehler (1992), Argentieri emphasizes that the adult's capacity to love "depends not only on how the oedipal drama has been resolved, but also on how the process of differentiation between self and object has developed". She later goes on to say that the person who acts out incest in real life is incapable of acknowledging the other person as such. In my clinical experience as director of a Centre for Psychotherapy for Children and Adolescents[1] who have suffered sexual abuse or incest, I think that the difficulty in accepting otherness is a crucial factor in the psychopathology of incestuous parents and can be classified as one of the severe forms of narcissistic disorders. This perspective, it seems to me, can generate a condensed integration of several theories, depending on whether we emphasize the vicissitudes of the drives, ego-centred psychology, the psychology of the self or the psychology of object relations.

In the severe psychopathological pattern of the incestuous family, the expansive narcissism of the abusive genitor produces a massive attack on oedipal triangulation and wipes out the vertices that designate the various *loci* designated by the terms: father, mother, son, daughter.

If, as Bataille (1957) maintains, transgression lifts a prohibition without suppressing it, incest is not a simple violation of the prohibition of incest. It is as though the prohibition had no value as representation for the abusive parent. That is what the twenty-two-year-old patient, Y, is in fact telling his analyst, in Simona Argentieri's example, when he says that during his childhood he received his father's "visit" at night, and then in daytime life carried on in an apparently normal fashion. In other words, incest is not only traumatic because of the transgression involved and its resultant effect on the psyche, it is also an attempt "to drive the other person crazy" because the incestuous parent disqualifies the child's perception, denying the gravity of the ignominious act. Magritte, who in one of his paintings represented the image of a pipe, added the comment "This is not a pipe", in order to emphasize the gap between a thing itself and its image or representation. When incestuous genitors, who do not have the aesthetic talent of the Belgian artist, actually carry out the act, they send a paradoxical message to the child: "this is not incest", thereby stitching together the fantasy representation and the transgressive act itself. The effect is a double traumatic impact.

An adult patient, whom I will call F, said that when she was twelve years old she had been deflowered by her father, who had introduced his fingers into her vagina. In doing so, the father had not used gloves. This detail is important, since he was a gynaecologist. The incestuous act had taken place in his office. The father had performed those digital penetrations in the name of medicine and "the necessary knowledge a gynaecologist must have of a woman's body, even though she may be his daughter". This type of incest was repeated over the years, during which the transgression and its negation were superimposed.

The incestuous family finds it impossible to accept otherness as such. From the outside, the family group looks as though it consists of several members. But from the point of view of its mental functioning, there are no limits or boundaries to separate them. Such families operate as if the group was Hydra-like, with only one body but many heads. Expressed as an equation, its functioning would take the form: $1 + 1 + 1 = 1$ and not 3.

When an incestuous father uses his daughter's body to obtain a certain type of sexual pleasure, he negates her as a person, as a self distinct from him. In a relationship that I would define as narcissistic–omnipotent, this is the sense in which the father (or mother) abuses the child: the child's status as a separate self is denied.

Thus, for example, the incestuous father of an adolescent girl expressed his fear that his daughter might be sexually assaulted whenever she went out of doors, saying "*if anything should happen to me . . . er . . . her . . .*" That slip of the tongue reveals the non-differentiation that governed their relationship.

The incestuous act negates the fact that all human beings are necessarily "incomplete". It is a desperate attempt to avoid confronting—something we all must do—ambivalence and loss of the object. Denying that the irreducible existence of the other is *per se* a source of conflict for the ego, incest seeks to evacuate all conflict through the suppression of all otherness.

In their attempt to achieve these ends, the perpetrators do not hesitate to obliterate the child's desire and, consequently, thinking, leaving him or her mentally bewildered, the inevitable effect of the accumulation of trauma. Such children are forced into a paradoxical form of immobilization; their silence is perhaps a reflection of the representational nothingness into which they are sucked. In its narcissistic expansion, the megalomanic ego of the incestuous parents engulfs the other person, seen as a mere extension of themselves. The desire of the one is incompatible with that of the other. In their "totalizing utopia", incestuous parents experience themselves as having mastery over time and death. In their wish to throw their net over the child, they try to ignore the fact that the object, by virtue of his or her essential nature, real or fantasized, creates a conflicting relationship with the ego. The ego of the incestuous parent aims to entrap the object, but in so doing robs the other person of all vitality (Tesone, 1998).

> A female patient, who had for years been subjected to an incestuous type of relationship with her father, had the following dream, which reveals both the relationship of merging and non-differentiation in which she found herself and her attempt to escape from it: "My father is holding me by the arm, I try to break loose but I can't. Then I bite his arm with all my strength, and suddenly I wake up. Actually, I was biting my own arm, so hard in fact that once I woke up, I could still see the teeth marks on it."

Narcissism—writes Green (1979)—sustains the illusion that a no-Oedipus situation (not anti-Oedipus but non-Oedipus) can exist in so far as it knows only the ego/I. "Like God, the ego considers itself self-created, without sex, that is, without sexual limits and without filiation, and therefore without kinship structure."

The incestuous sexual relationship is necessarily a form of masturbation, because here sexuality remains auto-erotic in the sense that it is played out as though the other person had no existence. The child's only function is to satisfy this object auto-eroticism. Paraphrasing M. de M'Uzan (1965), quoted by Couvreur (1995), I would say that there is a "spectrum of identity" between the abusive genitor and the abused child. In this case, there is no object-related libido as such; where ordinarily there would be two poles, that of the object-related libido and that of its narcissistic counterpart, with a to-and-fro movement between the two, here the situation is very much like what M. de M'Uzan describes as tension between two kinds of narcissistic libido: an "intra-ego" one and an "extra-ego" one.

There is an excellent example of this particular disposition of the libido in the patient Simona Argentieri calls V, who was afraid of giving in to her incestuous impulses with her daughter through masturbation. This fantasy is concomitant with a regressive dimension of being sucked in by her own mother, for whom the "third person" of the oedipal triangle was excluded.

The myth of the Unique, that is, the illusion of being an omnipotent being without defect, is a fantasy shared by most abusive parents. Their children exist only as appendages to an ego that delights in its own grandiosity. The child has no value *per se* other than that of a narcissistic adjunct. The incestuous attempts of the abusive parent could be represented as a triangle, the vertices of which remain unclosed, set within a circumscribing circle (Tesone, 1994). In other words, through their expansionist utopia, abusive parents intend to undo the vertices of the oedipal triangle, encircling it within their megalomania of the Unique. Between the abusive father and his young daughter, there is no relationship like that between self and object; the disappearance of the object leaves only a relationship within the self. Here we find ourselves involved in a fantasy of the existence of a Double, the guarantee of narcissistic completeness.

The desperate quest of incestuous parents is often motivated— as Simona Argentieri emphasizes—by confusion between masculine and feminine, and the impossibility to mourn the loss of androgyny.

In his famous article on the confusion of tongues between children and adults, Ferenczi (1932) highlights the fact that confusion arises precisely when the adult responds to a request for tenderness from the child with the language of eroticization. The child's initial reaction, says Ferenczi, is one of rejection, hate, disgust, and violent resistance. However, when the intimidation persists, the aggressor is introjected and disappears as a figure in external reality. The aggressor feels no guilt, since guilt is projected into the child. And the child, by introjecting the guilt feelings evacuated by the adult, later demands punishment. Incest, as Simona Argentieri emphasizes, "constructs a complicated and complex architecture of guilt, ubiquitous in the case of the unconscious fantasy, and, paradoxically, inequitably distributed in cases where incest has actually been carried out".

This guilt often leads children who have experienced an incestuous relationship to have accidents repeatedly or even actually attempt suicide; these are expressions of the internal need for punishment.

Confusion, identification with the aggressor, guilt, lack of confidence in the child's own perception, feelings of shame (especially as regards anything that involves the body) are the effects in the boy or girl of the incestuous act.

As Simona Argentieri reminds us, good and evil, what is good and what is bad—and therefore the feeling of guilt—remain in an area of confusion similar to that of perverse states of mind. Children who have been subjected to incest, and Simona Argentieri's patient A is illustrative in this sense, desperately attempt to escape from the confusion between eroticization and tenderness, and seek "a protective function" as Argentieri demonstrates so well. In this quest, however, their lack of discrimination sometimes leads them, via the compulsion to repeat, to put themselves in situations where they are once again victims.

What is the dominant affect in the incestuous relationship? In my view, hate supported by the death drive impregnates the relationship, which is, in fact, a non-relationship—or perhaps a type of archaic relationship in which love is not differentiated from hate in its effects. Eroticization aims to conceal the thanatic dimension, but all it achieves is the exclusion of any notion of line of descent: there are neither offspring nor ancestors, neither origin nor posterity. The incestuous act denies the fact of exclusion from the primal scene and aims at its destruction (if there is no primal scene, there is no exclusion).

Incest today

Argentieri asks whether the increased tolerance of atypical expressions of sexuality in contemporary society might tend to trivialize the incestuous act. McDougall (1995) speaks not of perversions but of neo-sexualities, that is, the many ways of expressing sexuality that both hetero- and homosexual adults may enjoy. McDougall reserves the term "perversion" for sexual relations that are imposed by one individual on another who does not consent to it or is not able to give consent because of his or her age. To this degree of trivialization, according to Simona Argentieri, we might add a

certain deficiency in parenting functions, with the consequent difficulty in imposing norms and limits. Argentieri proposes an attrac-
tive hypothesis when she suggests that what is undergoing such
radical change is not the oedipal milestone as such but the defences
that are employed against its integration. According to Simona
Argentieri, in our psychoanalytic practice we are increasingly
having to deal with mechanisms of splitting and disavowal, instead
of the classic repression, or even with primitive states of mind
governed by non-integration, confusion, and ambiguity. Would
incest evoke less horror for these reasons? It is difficult to find an
unequivocal answer, although I hope that by the end of this symposium we may be more able to answer that question. Simona
Argentieri is perfectly justified in questioning the term "abuse",
widely used today. It has come to include incest, thanks to the
subtlety of contemporary language, one consequence of which is to
lessen the dramatic impact of the term "incest" itself. I would add:
if only "abuse" is prohibited, does this imply that "use" is not? An
ambiguity that had best be avoided. This is why I agree with
Simona Argentieri that we would do well to drop this term whenever we are referring to incest. I prefer to use the term "incestuous
sexual violence", which unambiguously emphasizes its thanatic
quality.

Simona Argentieri asks if the cultural and psychological barrier
against incest is crumbling in contemporary society. It is not easy to
find an answer to that question. I believe that what has occurred, as
a consequence of contemporary interest in the human rights of children, is the removal of the taboo of silence. A problem hitherto
banished from thought, negated, silenced, has become thinkable; it
can be put into words and therefore be thought of as existing. I
would say that the apparent increase in frequency is actually an
increased capacity to conceive of incest as existing; it therefore
becomes able to estimate its prevalence in quantitative terms, something that has been negated until now.

To conclude, I will refer briefly to the myth of Narcissus (Grimal,
1976). There are three versions:

(a) In Ovid, Narcissus is loved by the nymph Echo, who, when
     Narcissus rejects her, goes off on her own; only a plaintive
     voice can be heard. Narcissus, after a day's hunting, goes

down to a lake to slake his thirst, falls in love with his own image (which he does not recognize) and, leaning too far over, disappears into the water.

(b) In Boethius, a young man falls in love with Narcissus. Narcissus gives him his sword, with which the young man commits suicide. After this, the scene at the lake is the same as in version (a).

(c) In Pausanias, Narcissus has a twin sister. On her untimely death, Narcissus suffers unbearable pain. This pain disappears fleetingly one day when, contemplating himself in a lake, Narcissus believes he sees his sister's image.

In his interpretation of this myth, Nathan (1984) underlines the fact that Narcissus seems to abandon his suitors. But this is actually not so; on the contrary, Narcissus attempts to be reunited with them but "in a way that creates confusion between subject and object".

The three versions, writes Nathan,

> have a common denominator: they evoke, each in its own specific register, Narcissus's attempt to be in one place and in its opposite, to be both emitter and receptor of his own voice, active and passive, man and woman, and yet still himself. To re-find, to love, to join with, or to be merged with his double of the opposite sex (or of the other world) is the taboo that Narcissus violates.

The Double, says Menahem (1995), cannot be considered to be a return of the repressed; it is the sudden emergence of something unthinkable and non-represented.

Is the horror of the incestuous act a response simply to the transgression of the prohibition of incest, or does it cover at the same time the transgression of the narcissistic taboo, thereby multiplying its devastating effect?

From the oedipal milestone to narcissistic mirror-images? As Baranes (1995) emphasizes, it seems that Oedipus must quite often give up his place on our psychoanalytic couches in favour of Narcissus, just as happens in the social and cultural domains. The prevalence of Narcissus over Oedipus is what characterizes incest, but perhaps it also generates the change in defensive modes witnessed in contemporary psychoanalytic practice, creating the impression that actually performing the incestuous act is a much more frequent occurrence than in the past.

Note

1. Centre Médico-Psycho-Pédagogique E. Pichon-Rivière, 9 Cour des Petites-Écuries, 75010 Paris.

CHAPTER THREE

Incest: the crushed fantasy

Monique Cournut-Janin

I n the beginning was the act, and the act was murder and incest. Psychoanalysis acknowledges how important these are for the Unconscious. Any civilizing influence or attempt at processing them mentally tends to end up in repression; yet they are still present in the life of each individual as in society itself, and they carry threats of destruction. Gang rapes are not incestuous . . . but can we be sure that, in the unconscious of those who perpetrate them, this is really the case?

In this paper, I shall concentrate on parent–child incest, leaving to one side any discussion of brother–sister incest—even though the latter easily lends itself not only to displacing and inflecting the prohibition but also to toning it down, since it does not transgress the difference between generations. I shall therefore give up any thought of wandering along the banks of the River Nile, following Isis as she tries to gather together the pieces of her husband and brother, Osiris. A fecund incest, that one, since from Horus, their divine son, the first of the Pharaohs was born . . .

It is, naturally enough, very difficult not to let oneself be influenced by myths about beginnings.

The origin of the universe is parthenogenetic. Gaia, the Earth, was born of Chaos, and then, again parthenogenetically, begot Uranus, the heavens. Uranus lay on top of her (the first recorded instance of sexual intercourse) and provided her with babies; but since he remained on top of her and kept penetrating her, these infants were unable to leave their mother's womb. So Gaia gave one of her sons, Cronus, still inside her, a billhook; he proceeded to castrate his father, thereby allowing his brothers and sisters to be born into the world. And so incest and castration appear as corner-stones, as Jean-Pierre Vernant's recent (1999) book shows so well. Incest and castration, acted out in mythology, give structure to the societies we establish and form the very basis of our unconscious.

In focusing simply—if I may put it thus—on incest, I would like to discuss some of its patterns. Let us follow the various protago-nists and cover the range of possibilities.

Father and daughter

Incest between father and daughter is the form that is best known and, it is claimed, the most widespread. I shall base my discussion on three sources: Freud, the anthropologists (though they will speak later), and finally my own experience in an adolescent walk-in centre.

(a) Freud and Katharina

Freud's case-report in "Studies on hysteria" (1895d) is beautifully written. Now that certain of Freud's letters have been made available to a wider public, the material has become even more meaningful— Freud was writing about how painful it felt to have a father who sex-ually abused one of Sigmund's brothers and one of his sisters.

The story is supposed to take place at a height of two thousand metres, in an inn. When the innkeeper's niece found out that Freud was a doctor, she decided to confide in him: she complained that she often felt out of breath. Freud soon came to realize that these were anxiety attacks. Gradually, in the course of her answers to Freud's questions, Katharina described those attacks in more detail: "I think all the time someone's standing behind me and going to catch hold of me all at once. [. . .] I always see an awful face that looks at me in a dreadful way, so that I'm frightened." In response to further questioning, Katharina told Freud when the attacks first began: two years before, while she was still living on the other mountain with her aunt—that was when she saw her uncle lying on top of Franziska, her cousin. Even though she "couldn't get [her] breath" and "everything went blank", Katharina told Freud that she did not at that time understand what was going on: "I was only sixteen. I don't know what I was frightened about." She went on: "I was so frightened that I've forgotten everything." She did, however, recall that she had felt sick continuously for three days afterwards. When Freud suggested that perhaps something had made her feel disgusted, Katharina described what happened after that: she reported her discovery to her aunt, there were some very disagree-able scenes between her uncle and her aunt as a result, and her aunt decided to move with her children and niece and take over the present inn—leaving her uncle alone with Franziska, who had meanwhile become pregnant, in the other inn.

At this point, Katharina began to tell Freud of two older stories, which went back two or three years earlier than the traumatic moment. She described how she had once gone with her uncle on an expedition and they had spent the night in an inn. She woke up suddenly "feeling his body" in the bed. According to Katharina, the following conversation ensued: "What are you up to, Uncle? Why don't you stay in your own bed?" Uncle: "Go on, you silly girl, keep still. You don't know how nice it is." "I don't like your 'nice' things; you don't even let me sleep in peace."

On an earlier occasion, Katharina had had to defend herself against him when he was completely drunk, and she told Freud of other incidents between her uncle and Franziska. "[Freud] asked her if she had been suspicious at that time. 'No, I didn't think anything about it; I only just noticed it and thought no more about it.'" Katharina seemed suddenly to have a feeling of relief. "At that time," Freud goes on, "she had carried about with her two sets of experiences which she remembered but did not understand, and, from which she drew no inferences. When she caught sight of the couple in intercourse, she at once established a connection between the new impression and these two sets of recollections, she began to understand them and at the same time to fend them off. There then followed a short period of working-out, of 'incubation' after which the symptoms of conversion set in, the vomiting [. . .]. She had not been disgusted by the sight of the two people but by the memory which that sight had stirred up in her. And, taking everything into account, this could only be the memory of the attempt on her at night when she had 'felt her uncle's body'." The "frightening head" that appeared during her attacks could then be linked to the sight of her uncle's face, "distorted with rage" because she had told her aunt what had been going on.

Incidentally, the wealth of theoretical opportunities with which this short clinical account provided Freud should not be forgotten. What he was many years later to call *Nachträglichkeit* (deferred action/*après-coup*) is clearly present here in his report, with the latency between two sets of experiences. The same is true of "splitting"—it was only in 1937 that Freud was able to see in this a metapsychological concept.

In a footnote that he added in 1924, Freud revealed that this had been in fact an attempted father–daughter incest: the man involved was Katharina's father, not her uncle.

We could surmise also that the brief encounter between Freud and Katharina had a cathartic effect: many years later, Winnicott was to talk of "therapeutic consultations".

(b) As regards this essentially paradigmatic pattern—incest between father and daughter—in the *socius* as well as in the Unconscious, various different permutations would appear to be possible.

The most widespread is an exchange of daughters between fathers—and here we find ourselves close to issues such as exogamy and the attempt to ensure that more women are "available", as Lévi-Strauss described the situation in *The Elementary Structures of Kinship* (1969). These issues had already been discussed by Mauss (1950) and, more recently, by Godelier (1996). I do not wish to go into these aspects more fully, since my aim in this paper is much more modestly clinical in outlook.

(c) Some years ago, a walk-in centre for adolescents was set up in Paris. Open twenty-four hours a day, 365 days a year, it took in any youngster who felt that he or she was going through a particularly rough time. Parents would be contacted only after the adolescent agreed, and the youngster would be allowed to stay in the facility until some kind of start could be made in processing his or her problems, first with us, then, if possible, with the parents.

Often sexual issues would be at the root of the problems these adolescents were trying to cope with.

I shall begin by discussing the three types of what Racamier (1995) called "incestual" response that the fathers of these youngsters manifested.

Crossover identification between father and daughter

This youngster was a plump little girl, still very childlike in appearance. She had taken refuge in the walk-in centre because she had found herself trapped in a quite incredible situation. She would leave school after classes, chatting away to her friends. Her father, who was worried the local yobbos might take too close an interest in his daughter, was very strict about the time by which she should be home from school. How could she avoid being punished? She made up an excuse . . . along the exact lines of what her father had been imagining: a man had followed her and she had had to take the long way round to get rid of him . . . Her father told the police, and was even more strict as to the time by which she was to be back home. On one particular day, she completely forgot what time it was, she had gone to a friend's house with a group of girls to have an afternoon snack. She arrived home three hours late. . . . Panic-stricken, she told her father (had she seen something like it on TV or heard it on the radio?) that she had been kidnapped by several men who had smothered her mouth and nose with a wad of cotton-wool, and that she had woken up much later, all alone in the dark. Driven out of his wits by anxiety and rage, her father—who not for a moment questioned the slightest detail of what she had told him—began to accompany her every day to and from school: she was left with no breathing space at all. One day she did manage to break free . . .

When she arrived at the walk-in centre, we were struck by the incongruity between her childlike face and speech, and the strangely titillating women's clothes she was wearing—black leather mini-skirt, fishnet stockings, a well-cut leather jacket. When we met her father, a whole new perspective was opened up—the way the daughter was dressed was a mirror image of his own clothing (with the addition of the fishnet stockings): he wore leather trousers and a leather jacket. He dressed her in clothes like his, hence her unconsciously provocative demeanour with respect to men, the very thing that, consciously, he wanted so much to prevent. His unconscious homosexuality, projected on to his daughter dressed in the way she was (and she was not even pubertal), was thus put on display for other men to look at.

Was the mother excluded from this relationship? Was she depressed? We never met her, and the very least I can say is that she really was absent, both as regards what the daughter had to tell us and in the father's remarks.

The daughter functioned in one or other of two modes: in the one, appropriate for her age and for her mental/physical development, she was a not-yet-pubertal girl; in the other, she was identified with her father's unconscious desire. The arrangement the father had come to with respect to his instinctual drives said it all too clearly (though he himself did not realize it): "I'm keeping my eye on her; I'm not going to let those bastards fuck *me*" . . .

The waitress and the customers

This time we really are dealing with an adolescent girl. A waitress in her parents' cafe, she would often hear male customers make joking remarks to her; her father accused her of acting provocatively towards them, and threatened to have her locked up. When we spoke to her father on the phone, he yelled: "If she doesn't come home, I'll kill her"; her mother crowned that with a "If she doesn't come home, I'll kill myself". These two statements highlight the different nature of the involvement that each of the sexes experiences whenever parents try to come to terms with the explosion that occurs as their daughter reaches puberty. The father feels dispossessed, perhaps even directly called into question on a homosexual level via feminine identification; the mother feels guilty—what did she do or say that drove her daughter to jeopardize the equilibrium of the whole family?

To be a whore or not

She was eighteen and, without actually taking refuge there, she had come along to the walk-in centre on several previous occasions to confide in someone and talk about what she felt was her "destiny", fearing that it was gradually creeping up on her. Ever since puberty, when men began to glance at her as they passed her by in the street, she had been the target of her father's verbal abuse. His daughter's adolescence meant that he was henceforth having to deal with an intolerable situation: she was no longer "his" little girl, but a woman—and the glances that other men gave her confirmed the fact. Feeling dispossessed, he defended himself blindly against those counter-oedipal impulses that would have pushed him towards committing incest; but at the same time, he was jealous of any male who, in his imagination, might take possession of her. And so he kept on saying to his daughter that she would end up walking the streets, a prostitute—in a way, she would be a woman whom all the men the world could possess because he could not have her for himself alone. And the young woman, caught up in what seemed to function like an order, told me of her fear that she would "obey" him and really turn out to be a whore . . .

It is interesting to note that looks and glances are very much to the fore in these accounts—those that are directed at the daughter, as well as those of the fathers, imagining how other men are looking at their daughters.

In the case of these fathers, it would seem that, faced with the temptation of incest, they begin by regressing towards the anal phase in an attempt to keep their hold on the object (which thereupon seems to take on part-object features); beyond that, there is the emergent risk of feminine identification with the object, designated as desirable because of the looks that others direct towards it—and the temptation of feminine identification is, for the Unconscious, equivalent to castration. Though Freud wrote optimistically of "The dissolution of the Oedipus complex" (1924d), he did acknowledge that castration anxiety was always present in the Unconscious.

The adolescent girl's difficulties in coming to terms with the fact that she is henceforth an adult with the sexual identity of a woman are often highlighted. Less has been written about the work that adolescence requires the parents to do in their psyche.

It is a critical moment when a father sees that his daughter is henceforth a woman—and sees that fact confirmed in the glances that other men give her. When the years of latency have been shared together and the ties of tenderness are solid enough, it is easier to come to terms with that critical point in life. But when the realities of life have made living and sharing together impossible—with the result that those ties have never been properly established—it becomes much more difficult to process.

I feel it important to understand what lay behind these attitudes, even though they did not lead directly to incest.

On one occasion, however, in the walk-in centre, we had to deal with the consequences of an encounter between a truly perverse father (sexual perversion as well as perversity of character) and his daughter. This is how I would narrate the story.

A 17-year-old girl in a kind of drably-depressive state wanted the staff to help her find accommodation in a hostel. Her mother had died several years previously, and she lived with her father and two younger brothers. It proved very difficult to establish sufficient rapport and trust with her, but at last she was able to tell us, with feelings of shame and guilt, of her father's sexually interfering with her—every single night since she was a little girl, and even while her mother, though ill, was still alive. Some time ago—probably because she was gradually becoming aware of the fact that she was no longer a little girl but a grown woman—she had begun to refuse these nightly visits, though in fear and guilt. We were concerned for her because she seemed unable to say *why* she felt so guilty; she was no longer able to concentrate, to work properly . . . It was as though the burst of energy that had enabled her to put an end to her father's incestuous activity had left her completely helpless: splitting had meant that her father was both someone who had failed to obey a prohibition *and* the only parental support she had after her mother's death. Now that she had closed her bedroom door on him, he spoke to her with bitter irony, and she felt totally abandoned. This case left every member of staff with very painful memories. And this is the reason why.

We discussed matters with her father, and he agreed that she should be accommodated in a hostel—though he did so in an obviously rejecting way, sneering at "all this damsel-in-distress stuff"". She found it hard to adjust to life in the hostel . . . her father consulted a psychiatrist about her, who diagnosed a psychotic form of depression and decided to have her hospitalized in his own unit, a locked ward, where he bombarded her with neuroleptic medication. The contact we had with this psychiatrist convinced us that he was colluding with the father—who, as befits a very skilful pervert, had persuaded the psychiatrist that his daughter's complaints were delusional in nature and that he himself was a model father. In our conversations with the father, we became aware that he had never considered his daughter to be a whole object—she was no more than a fetish, a part-object of which he had possession and which, after her attempts to leave him, had turned into a faecal object good only for throwing away.

I wanted to present a case of acted-out incest between an adult and a child since there is always, in this kind of situation, a reference back to the original experience in which the child is seduced by the mother because of the everyday nursing care she provides: though this situation is common to everyone, it is processed differently in each of us in terms of how our states of mind are organized.

I think it important to come back to the consequences entailed by the polymorphously perverse disposition typical, as Freud argued, of infantile sexuality. Secondary repression, at the end of the oedipal phase, enables "normally-neurotic" future parents neither to see nor to hear the incestuous sexuality of their infant, and perhaps even to smile at it . . . a child, boy or girl, is just a child. For this to be the case, of course, there needs to be no serious parental pathology—of the kind I have just mentioned, for example, in the case of the perverse father.

I would suggest that the polymorphously perverse sexuality of our childhood is still within each and every one of us, more or less firmly repressed—and therefore more or less likely to be re-awakened by the ups and downs of life.

It should be remembered that the psychoanalytic setting as Freud defined it—with the analysand lying on the couch and the analyst out of sight—triggers a topographical regression that reactivates in the patient the representations and affects that were current when infantile sexuality was actively at work in his or her mind. The transference puts the psychoanalyst in a parental position with respect to the patient's childhood, so that any seduction by the analyst of the patient, male or female, is tantamount to the incestuous abuse *of a child*—the child who, in the trappings of an adult, is lying on the analytical couch.

Father–son incest

Moving on in our review of the various forms that incest may take, we come to incest between father and son. The story of Laius, who betrayed his host's hospitality by seducing the latter's son, is at the origin of the malediction that struck the Labdacids—the planned murder of a son, whose sacrifice was intended to prevent him from killing his paedophile father.

Festen, a Danish film, shows a son publicly—during a family celebration in honour of his father—accusing the latter of committing incest with him.

A patient once consulted me for his many phobias that left him almost completely unable to work. His behaviour disorder was posing a threat to the relationship he had succeeded in building up with a woman who was the mother of an adolescent girl. The patient felt persecuted by the obsessive sexual images that he was unable to put out of his mind whenever he and the girl happened to be together. In the work we did together, it proved difficult to overcome the violent dismissal with which the patient—who all the same knew perfectly well that he needed help—treated any attempt at understanding. It was only after a series of therapeutic consultations that he became able to talk about the masturbation sessions his father had imposed on him while he was still a very young boy—they stopped only when he became a high-school boarder in a neighbouring town. Later, he learned that his brother and sister had also been their father's victims.

Thanks to his analysis, this patient was able to overcome a considerable number of his phobias. The analytical transference gave rise to some very difficult moments—his fear of being sexually attacked by the analyst could at times be intensely experienced in the *hic et nunc* of the analytical process. That patient gives me reason to believe that, though it may seem to be difficult and painful, psychoanalysis in one or other of its forms—classic, case-appropriate setting, psychodrama, etc.—is an appropriate method for overcoming what has been experienced as a trauma that jeopardizes the patient's psychosexual development and the construction of his or her identity.

Incest between mother and child:

There are two possible forms of mother–child incest: mother–son and mother–daughter.

Freud described the general atmosphere of this type of incest in terms of the fourth primal fantasy, the return to the maternal womb. He emphasized too that in the development of infantile sexuality, the mother is the original seductress (because of the nursing care she gives her infant child)—I shall come back to this point in my discussion of mother–daughter incest.

Classically, mother–son incest is the one which has attracted the strongest prohibition; the mother–daughter pattern is still to a great extent unclear.

Mother–son incest

There have been several remarkable attempts to portray this form of incest—in literature, theatre, and film. *Jocasta and Oedipus*, Visconti's *The Damned*, Louis Malle's *Dearest Love* (known in the USA as *The Murmur of the Heart*) are perhaps the most direct and unadorned of these attempts. For the alienists in practice at the end of the nineteenth century, this form of incest could take place only within a *folie-à-deux* relationship.

That said, there is a wide range of possible arrangements for avoiding or circumventing this form of incest while retaining both the scent and the flavour of it—for every mother had a physical relationship in which she fondled, caressed, nursed and penetrated her child (boy or girl). Sons at least may be able to break free of these ties thanks to the eventuality of identifying with the father—and there is the fact that their genitals are different from the mother's: the penetrating penis. Daughters do not have such an outlet.

Mother–daughter incest

Can anything be said about this form of incest? Can it even be thought about? Yet, though it may not be thinkable, and cannot be put into words, it lies none the less at the very heart of all the other forms of incest, which, without exception, would seem to derive from it.

There may be something here that involves the return to an incestuous fusion as described by Christine Angot in her book *Incest* (1999). She writes first of all about the pangs and passions of a homosexual fusional relationship, and only *then* gives us a taste of what preceded it—the actual incestuous experience she had as a child with her father. It is of course true that paternal incest does not necessarily lead to homosexuality; but the mother–daughter relationship, with its identificatory reduplication of sameness, requires a paternal imago if breaking free of it is to be made possible. If this paternal imago is to separate the mother–child couple and de-sexualize it, it has to be reliable.

It was with respect to girls that Freud wrote of the pre-oedipal situation—the loving relationship with the mother that occurs so early in life and is so deeply buried in the psyche that analysing it is indeed a very difficult task. What trajectory must a young girl follow in order to leave this original love relationship behind her—one which, argued Freud, will influence every other such relationship that she may find herself in all through her life? To put it briefly, she has to move from fusion within an identical one-ness to separation and two-ness. Fain and Braunschweig (1975) highlight the need for the father's presence within the maternal psyche, one that has managed to pass through all stages of development, including the oedipal one: the presence of this third party has to be such that the infant—and here I am thinking in particular of the infant girl—can perceive it, so that auto-erotic practices can be established with the accompanying fantasy about the absent mother—absent because she is with the father. It is of course necessary for this position to be achieved that the crisis that every mother experiences when she gives birth to a child does not overwhelm her ability to process it.

The mother has to be one who designates the father as a love object, on condition that she forbids any genital sexuality with him: the mother alone is allowed to seduce him *with her genitals*. In this way, the mother protects herself and, for a time, protects her daughter against feelings of rivalry between two women; also, by designating the father as a love object, she offers her infant a means of separating from her.

Let us think for a moment about this idea. "Be seductive towards your father, but not with your genitals" or "Be completely phallic, not pierced—then you won't stir up your father's castration anxiety" (Cournut-Janin 1998). The risk of committing incest with the father is thus avoided—just as the most intense anxiety that the father could ever experience is diverted: buried deeply underneath castration anxiety is that of the *hole*.

I have suggested that it is this complicity, transmitted from mother to daughter, that should be called *femininity*: the female body has to be adorned, thereby displacing (in a fetishistic way) on to the body-as-a-whole the eroticism of genitals that have to remain hidden. This form of femininity requires a triangular relationship: it is set up and given structure "in the name of the father", of man.

What I would call the feminine sphere is, to my way of thinking, something quite different—more subtle, more secretive. It, too, is transmitted from one woman to another, under the disguise of femininity—a form of identification promising that one day, sometime in the future, the male genital organ and, later, a baby, will be found inside.

It is precisely at this juncture that there may be hiccups in the young girl's destiny. The primary bond of love, love for and of the mother, the body-to-body relationship, mouth-to-mouth, hole-to-hole, may well become stuck in that primitive kind of pattern, with no development possible. Being the maternal phallus thus seems to be an attempt to put into words, to represent within a phallic system what probably falls short of such a position. The physical, body-to-body relationship of some female homosexuals can teach us something about that—most of the time, there is no penetration, vagina and anus are excluded. Each duplicates the caresses of the other, "on the surface" as it were, with no facsimile of penile penetration. In short, no vagina and no penis.

In order to develop our understanding of how such a situation may come about, we have to go back to "normal" development. This includes, for both the infant girl and her mother, physical intimacy—which lasts for some considerable time—made up of caresses such that pride of place is given to the mother for everything reminiscent of feeding, nursing care, handling, cuddling.. For many a long year, all through the latency period in fact, the incestuous oedipal situation with its love for the father seems to be forgotten. It is as if the apparent return to one's original starting-point represented a secure "haven" just as much as the one proposed by Freud: it is the change of object, he argued—when the father is chosen—that represents a safe haven in the case of girls.

These two approaches can be reconciled if we follow what Freud wrote: each phase has not only its own specific rhythm but also its defensive strategies, even though these may be less obvious.

While the oedipal period is in full swing, love for the father is at its most passionate and the idea "When Mummy dies, I'll marry

Daddy" is very much a part of the young girl's thinking; in latency, deep-rooted identification with the mother, together with the absolute necessity that she exist—in as much as she is the primary object, her existence guarantees that of the girl herself—draws a veil over the sheer bluntness and cruelty of the death wishes the girl has for her mother once the father is chosen as the preferred object. That is why I refer to this latency intimacy between mother and daughter as a "safe haven"; the father's presence is not excluded for either of them. His daughter is a powerful attraction for him—but not with her genitals—as she snuggles into her mother's caressing arms. A state of affairs, of course, that cannot last for ever . . .

When this tripartite organization breaks down—for example, when all reference to the father is excluded—incest comes into mind: a mouth-to-mouth or hole-to-hole relationship from which what I have just called "femininity" is excluded.

The stumbling-blocks that psychoanalysts come across are less substantial: situations in which identification with the mother has proved impossible to achieve in a flexible and well-balanced way, with its accompanying object-related love. This has probably much more to do with maternal inclusion reminiscent of a melancholic nucleus that at times appears to function like a foreign body.

In such cases, there has been no repression of what may have been—indeed what almost certainly was—experienced as pleasure. Being washed, having baby lotion put on, being dried—all kinds of ecstatic pleasure arising not only from being fed, but also from excretion. As an adolescent (and perhaps even as an adult), the young woman finds herself caught up in a primitive world in which any possibility of separation, like any chance of acquiring her own self-identity, seems—to say the least—compromised.

> An adolescent girl who had run away from the hostel that she was stay-ing in sought refuge in our walk-in centre. Worn out, she was unable to say a word until someone mentioned her mother; as she spoke then of her childhood, her whole body began to jerk and shudder. When she was little, her mother used to put her into the care of some other person or institution for a few days, then take her back, again for a few days, before having her taken away again. That girl's body was illustrating, in a way that was to some extent (but not entirely) reminiscent of an hysterical representation, a maternal aspect that she had incorporated,

an aspect in which the accumulation of presence-and-absence gave her no opportunity to build up any personal consistency, any personal *locus* and space for fantasy inside her that had not been invaded by her mother. It is the opportunity to fantasize that prepares a feminine mind–body for the wish to be penetrated by a male genital organ and to nurture a child.

Since I have deliberately chosen in this paper to discuss ambiguous situations and incestual areas, I must mention one particular example that occurs frequently in our clinical practice when our patients have to come to terms with the fact that their parents are growing old.

Lapsing into second childhood

Several of my female patients have had to cope with their mother's physical and mental deterioration. Growing old means running the risk of "lapsing into second childhood", as everyday usage puts it— in other words, re-connecting in a backward-looking way with babyish inclinations and behaviour, playing around with genitality or even anality.

The eroticized exposing of the body, which occasionally goes together with encopresis, may, in a brutal reversal of the status quo, force a daughter to become the mother of her own mother who has "lapsed" into second childhood. By arousing drive-related impulses that have been repressed for so long, this situation may be experienced as something akin to an ambivalent rejection accompanied by intense feelings of guilt. And it really is a matter of a coming-together between mother and daughter that is experienced by the latter as sexually intolerable—a kind of incest that dare not say its name. Life's phases, the contact with previous and future generations, just as much as with one's collaterals, oblige each and every one of us, in our mental development, to process experiences that are more or less complex, in order to maintain some sort of equilibrium between the desire to merge with the other person and the wish to achieve independence. Except in cases of perversion, all this is marked by guilt feelings.

The infant's primary passivity and the refusal of anything that might bring it back echo the refusal of femininity in both sexes, as well as the demand for control and domination over oneself as well as the other person. The deviations that may arise are well documented; I have, in this paper, discussed some of them. Sometimes it is no longer a matter of deviation, but of destroying the other person who is experienced as "different", as "other": child, woman, Jew, Muslim, Black, White, Yellow . . . A tidal-wave carrying all of us in its wake, that the discovery of the death instinct enables us, if not to understand, at least to imagine: projecting an image of waste matter on to other people as a group, in order to strip them of their names, to banish them from the domain of words and thoughts, and propel them beyond death into something inanimate.

CHAPTER FOUR

Incest: a therapeutic challenge

Estela V. Welldon

I n this chapter I shall describe some of the most important aspects of incest as experienced during my clinical practice for over thirty years at the Portman Clinic, part of the Tavistock Portman National Health Service Trust in London. These include family dynamics, the clinical differences between incest perpetrators and paedophiles, the emotional consequences of father–daughter incest, the acknowledgement of maternal incest, the transferential and countertransferential responses from the professionals involved and the relevance of group analytical treatment for both victims and perpetrators of incest.

Family dynamics, acknowledgment, disclosure, secrecy

The importance of the *reality* of family dynamics in incest can hardly be overstressed, but somehow this has not always been acknowledged, since it was shadowed by a marked adherence to the seduction theory with its emphasis on unconscious fantasies. MacCarthy (1982) clearly and courageously stated:

I think it is a criticism of the contribution of Psychoanalysis to Psychiatry and allied professions that locating the theme of incest in the world of unconscious fantasy deflected attention away from the reality of incest and delayed the discovery of sexual abuse within the family.

The evolution of an incest situation goes through many stages. Typically it begins with a masked breakdown of the family structure, which perhaps is not consciously felt by any of its members. There may be, or appear to be, some specific events that, when they come to light later on, are identified as "causes" of incest. Incest operates on a number of different levels simultaneously in different family members including: a discharge of tension between both partners; a degree of satisfaction and sexual gratification where the child is easily available and can be seduced, always in a secretive manner. There is also in the case of father–daughter or stepdaughter incest, a discharge of intense hostility and revenge directed towards the female partner, in the person of her child. Incest provides, through some sort of emotional and physical "scaffolding", a re-establishment of some balance in the family dynamics. Later on, when disclosure makes its appearance it heralds its ending, since incest is no longer necessary to the family dynamics (Welldon, 1988).

It is very important to notice the family circumstances when the facts are disclosed. Is the wife over her depression, or her mourning period? Is she able to be "present" now? Has she resumed sexual intercourse with her husband? Or has another daughter become aware that her sister is the "favourite one" and so felt undermined? Is this the moment at which another sibling suffering from intense jealousy towards the incest victim denounces father and sister? As a matter of fact the study of the timing of the "disclosure time" and its effects in all family members could act as an accurate indicator of the many layers and their contents that have been hidden away for a long time. This could also serve as criteria for prognosis and treatment.

The importance of these dynamics have not always been recognized. Professional workers, especially in the past, have often made incredulous or sceptical remarks about a mother's denial of any knowledge that paternal incest had occurred. Such attitudes are not conducive to accurate diagnosis of the family dynamics. The mother in these cases cannot acknowledge the incest because temporarily she is emotionally and/or physically unable to respond to the demands placed on her as a mother, caretaker, wife, and partner. She is too depressed, detached, or exhausted to accept and fulfill her "duties". She can no longer cope. Bitter comments are made about mothers who knew, but didn't know. Some disbelieve their daughters; others ill-treat them when confronted with the reality. At other times, when mother is on the threshold between not knowing and knowing (something like a twilight zone) she is able to hear and acknowledge what is going on, and then she may call upon outside help, from general practitioners, social services, the law, the police. But there must be many cases which remain secret.

I have heard from many male patients who have committed incest how much they have felt rejected by their wives, and also been made to feel small, humiliated, and inadequate just as they did when they were young children with a very possessive, domineering, or neglectful mother. A period of impotence towards their wife can be a clinical indication that the incest is about to begin. In quite a number of cases this relates to the wife's new pregnancy and labour, or depression. The patient usually talks about his wife's coolness, distancing, and frigidity, and describes her as not wanting to have sex with him. He feels unable to pursue any extramarital affairs, indeed he claims he has never dreamt of being unfaithful to his wife. He even talks about incest as "keeping sex in the family" (to him this seems to be less of a betrayal of his wife than were he to go outside the family), and there is no cynicism attached to this statement. The "solution" in these cases, especially for a couple in which there is some emotional deprivation and lack of communication, seems to be the seduction of a child.

I remember a male patient, Keith, of whom I shall be talking more later on, who had maintained sexual relationships with his stepdaughter for five years, starting when the girl was six. His attraction towards her started when his wife became pregnant and refused to have sex with him. He felt able to contain his sexual urges, to wait until after the baby's birth and the readjustment of the family situation. A few months later when the baby died a cot death, his wife became deeply depressed and unable to meet his sexual requirements. The baby's short life had been a very stormy period, with daily fights between the parents. After the baby's death the husband withdrew, but was unable to express any feelings of grief. Instead, he suddenly felt prompted from within to approach his stepdaughter sexually. He did not know why he did it, except that he was in great need of warmth, care, and human contact. In his own words: 'It occurred to me that it might be preferable to approach my girl since she is part of the family and very much part of myself." During treatment he became aware of his intense anger, his own very low sense of self-esteem, and his wish for revenge against his wife as represented by her daughter. The situation had been complicated by the fact that he had secretly accused his wife of the baby's death, which happened one night when he was away from home after a fight. He was projecting his own guilt on to his wife, since in his view the baby would not have died had he been there. He also observed his own inability to mourn his child, and his manic defence in abusing the child who had survived.

Secrecy

Sometimes the "secret" of incest has been hidden away for years and years. When patients involved in incest situations are very cautious in making critical remarks about their parents or early life history ("everything was just normal, absolutely fine"), their statements should not necessarily be taken as true. If we listen carefully for what has been omitted from their own histories, incidents usually emerge which point to an early traumatic event or events that occurred when they were small. In other cases, when there is an apparent lack of memory about early childhood events in people who have committed or have been involved in sexual offences, it may be fruitful to investigate further to see whether they have blocked off episodes from early childhood that are too painful to recall. This could be particularly relevant for the incest victim's mother, who not infrequently turns out to have been an incest victim herself.

I repeat that secrecy, especially in paternal incest, is at the core of the situation: each member of the family is involved, whether "knowing" or "unknowing", but nobody talks about it. Indeed, it is irrelevant when paternal incest has occurred whether mother acknowledges the possibility of incest or not; had she been able to acknowledge it in the first place, incest would never have happened. Incest is committed in an effort to create ties to "keep the family together". Secrecy is the new taboo that has emerged from the breakdown of the taboo against incest (Ciba Foundation, 1984, p. 13). Nobody "knows" about it, or rather nobody acknowledges it.

Long term consequences of father–daughter incest

Sometimes the daughter unconsciously colludes in the incest, not only because of her father's demands but also because she is responding to her mother's inability to cope. That is why most girls report their fathers' sexual assaults on them only when the father takes another daughter for this "duty". The first girl then feels debased and betrayed, not so much because her position as her father's favourite is being usurped but because she is no longer the one chosen to fulfil this "duty" for her mother. Before the incest, she felt her mother did not understand her and she longed to get closer to her. Sometimes, she has even become her own mother's mother in an effort to create some sense of intimacy with her. So incest, if this is required, seems inevitable.

Incest gives much and then takes everything away, all at once. The little girl is now supposed to have all that she could have dreamt of in her wildest unconscious fantasies, including her father as her lover. And what does this situation bring for her? She shares a secret with Daddy that nobody knows about. Her dreams have become true. Now she has Daddy's love, penis, and the lot. And she is left in utter misery, with a complete lack of trust in anyone. Those who were supposed to look after her, and to keep firm boundaries between her worlds of fantasy and reality, have failed her, and all is now confusion. She has an enormous sense of loneliness. Such girls have difficulties in acknowledging any angry feelings because these feelings are extremely intense. They feel angry with their mother, whom they see as having failed to protect them, and angry with their father because he has abused them. As a patient of mine said, "I hate women and distrust men." They have been left with deep scars that will have a marked impact not only on their emotional lives, but also on all their physical relationships, since they often feel that the only way to gain love is through sexualization.

It is my suggestion that girls who have been victims of incest see very few alternatives to prostitution upon reaching adulthood. In any event, their bodies will respond in a massive way, either with an exaggeration of the libido or with completely repressed sexuality. Their severe problems range from prostitution to chronic psychosomatic symptoms. In my work over thirty years I have observed acute psychopathology, but have not encountered more positive outcomes such as the absence of sexual or emotional conflicts arising in adulthood in incest survivors.

The two damaging effects, promiscuity and sexual coldness, might seem to be complete opposites, but there are strong connections: I have often encountered women who are promiscuous, or have been involved in promiscuity, whose problems are related to sexual coldness. More often than not promiscuity is accompanied by frigidity and prostitution by sexual coldness, which leads to promiscuous behaviour and perverse sexual fantasies.

Let's start with the "prostitution solution". The disparity in statistics reveals a confused picture, but one which corresponds to the nature of the problem—the secrecy surrounding incest. In the dynamic process of incest, girls have learnt how to keep to themselves important and intimate secrets. This knowledge is turned into primitive defence mechanisms such as splitting and denial. Their "knowing it all" and their tendency to self-sacrifice, flamboyancy, and self-destructiveness could be bitterly exploited in adulthood for the "excellence" of this "new trade". It is well known that most incest survivors "may attract later on in life sexually aggressive and demanding partners" (Ciba Foundation, 1984, p. 16). Are those early acquired "skills" determining their fate?

At other times, they develop severe chronic psychosomatic pathology which renders medical practitioners unable to make proper diagnostic recommendations and to effect proper treatment. Such was the case with Patricia, who for seventeen years had experienced much somatic pain for which she sought radical treatment. She was fortunate enough that her general practitioner did not collude with her wish to damage her body even further with inadequate "treatments". Eventually the mystery was solved when she found the courage to tell him that she had been a victim of paternal incest for fifteen years, since the age of thirteen. She had tried successfully to erase this from her mind but she had not succeeded to do the same with her body.

Differences between incest perpetrators and paedophiles

Within the understanding of the family context it is important to make a differential diagnosis between incest perpetrators and paedophiles in order to make accurate risk assessments and treatment recommendations.

Incest may be the outcome of dysfunctional family dynamics, often including an external event, such as a pathological bereavement. Paedophiles, though, do not present significant changes in their behaviour towards children related to external circumstances. They present an early history of being both neglected and physically overwhelmed by the carer figure (usually the mother) with whom they still feel a very strong bond and a great deal of dependency. In their inner lives they are still small children who "justifiably" in their fantasies and acting out can make "legitimate" couplings with another small child. They also see themselves as "carers" of that child, but can not help treating them as part-objects, just as they were treated themselves in their early lives.

While both groups, incest perpetrators and paedophiles, involve themselves in child abuse and have had a traumatic early childhood, their presenting problems and surrounding circumstances are quite different. Incest perpetrators have been able to achieve a fully developed relationship with another adult and to have a family. In contrast, paedophiles target primarily under-age children, male or female, and they are not engaged in adult relationships. Incestuous fathers shift from wife to offspring, whereas paedophiles target women for their offspring. Furthermore, paedophiles have intense fears of relating to their peer group—men and women. Their attitude towards the children involved is marked by intense externalization, rationalization, and justification of their actions, making themselves believe that initiation to sexuality by adults is a healthy process. Paedophiles also claim to be completely unaware of the serious, long- and short-term consequences involved to the children they have abused. Instead, incestuous parents are usually more aware of the long-term consequences produced by their actions, especially when they are taken into therapy. Attitude towards treatment is also different. Incestuous parents are often more motivated and frequently we see couples who come for treatment because of their incipient awareness of their need for understanding and professional help. This is a rather unusual, if ever found, characteristic in paedophiles. In practical terms risk assessment and dangerousness are quite different for both groups; so far as the two categories do not overlap (as sometimes could happen). Incestuous fathers, on the whole, do not present future danger to other children, while paedophiles, often, regardless of treatment and management could still offer future danger to children in general.

Incest perpetrators, if properly assessed and treated, have a better prognosis than paedophiles.

Acknowledgement of maternal incest, is it Oedipus or Jocasta?

Do mothers commit incest more frequently than we think and more at the mother's initiative than we imagine?

Are we blocked from perceiving this by our idealization of motherhood? Surely we are, and this is why even in the original oedipal situation we fail to notice Jocasta's responsibility. Hers is the most important case of incest (Welldon, 1988).

Typically, we have always blamed Oedipus and not his mother. Here we are once more attaching the sole responsibility to the male child and consequently developing a whole new concept of a complex, taking it for granted that Oedipus unconsciously "knew" his mother, and was behaving perversely by marrying her. In fact, Jocasta was far better equipped, even consciously, to recognize Oedipus as her son than vice versa. She was the only one to know that Oedipus could be alive, as opposed to Laius, who believed him dead. Why do we not charge her with, if not all, at least a large share of the responsibility for enacting her own incestuous desires? It is clear that, if not perverse herself, she had associated with a most perverse individual, her husband Laius, who was a paedophile, his most important reason for not wanting children. She not only married him, already giving signs of being the willing victim of a perverse partnership (the clinical analogy still applies), but contrived to get him drunk in order to get herself impregnated. In other words, she already knew her own power as the master of her own offspring, even to the extent of giving him away at birth. She might unconsciously know that she—or indeed he, the offspring— could pursue the lost relationship, the power of motherhood later being replaced by that of incest, which would be more rewarding for her.

It seems unnecessary for researchers to develop a parallel Electra complex to the oedipal one, when Jocasta already fulfils that role. Is this again an obstinate tendency to see women as the weak sex, always the victims and never the perpetrators of sexual assault? It has always been made to appear that women are incapable of effecting their own perverse sexual designs in a skilful and masterly way, with young boys reckoned to be the only ones to enact sexual fantasies. I believe that many theories concerning female sexual development are misguided. This might have been born partly of a need to see an "earth mother" operating at all times, a woman who has been so idealized, or perhaps even idolized, that her faults are overlooked. She is portrayed as powerless in the penis-envy dilemma or, according to the new feminists, the victim of social attitudes, even perhaps contemptible because of her seeming less importance than the male. It looks as though we have all become silent conspirators in a system in which, from whatever angle we look at them, women are either dispossessed of all power, or made the sexual objects and victims of their male counterparts. We do not attribute to them any sense of responsibility for their own unique functions, deeply related to fecundity and motherhood, and liable at times to manifest themselves perversely. Why is it that Jocasta, when both she and Oedipus learn the facts of their incestuous relationship, promptly commits suicide? Apparently Oedipus cannot at first grasp the situation. The truth must therefore have been much closer to Jocasta's consciousness.

On countless occasions, agencies and establishments have expressed alarm, sometimes verging on panic, when referring male patients to me as sexual abusers. This contrasts strongly with the difficulty my female patients have often had in being taken seriously by some agencies. The few women who eventually refer themselves to me for treatment do so because all their previous attempts to get caring attention for their feelings of being too close, emotionally and physically, to their child, whether boy or girl, were not really taken seriously. I have noticed that mothers are more ready to report incestuous feelings and actions towards their daughters than towards their sons. In the latter case, one does not hear until much later, and then usually from the son's history.

In this context, I remember a patient of mine who was originally referred from a Child Guidance Clinic where her daughter, aged six, had been sent because of behavioural problems mainly related to school refusal. Following diagnostic assessment there, it was decided that the little girl's problems were the result of a very disturbed and difficult family situation, particularly in her relationship with her mother.

> My patient was described as an inadequate mother who showed intense exhibitionistic behaviour, such as exaggerating her physical demonstrations of affection towards her daughter. However, when she decided some time before to arrange a consultation for herself because of these preoccupations, she was told not to worry: "It is just natural for a mother to feel very fond of her children, especially if they are single parents". She had so closely identified with her daughter that she had come to act like a little girl, expecting her daughter to take complete care of her needs, including being cuddled and bathed by her. The little girl defended herself against these excessive demands by a most primitive and infantile acting out.

> Mother and daughter had created a symbiotic relationship to the extent of sharing the same bed. The mother had initiated the girl in active sexual incest that involved caressing of breasts and eventually masturbation of her daughter's genitals. The mother had not allowed the girl to attend school because she could not bear the idea of her being away. Nor would the mother let her have her own friends, or life, or allow her to grow up. My patient explained: "I want to be the mother I never had, someone who could be all the time with me and whose attentions could be entirely devoted to me as her daughter instead of being like my mother, hating me so much for being a girl and so involved with the other children and her husband that she never had a minute for me alone. She never forgave me either, that I was born a girl, being the first child. She had so much longed for a boy. I was always the victim of humiliation, and it became much worse when all the other children, five, were born. They were all girls. Then my mother turned to me with

even more hatred than ever and my father began to approach me sexually. As soon as I could I emigrated to this country with the purpose of making my own life as a woman." From the moment of arrival she pursued prostitution as a profession that could leave her free all day long to be with her daughter. I saw her for a diagnostic appraisal when she was still a practising prostitute.

There are many possible outcomes surfacing from being incest victims, from either maternal or paternal to boys or girls, but a frequent one is to suffer from a sexual perversion. In this context there are female patients who have suffered from sexual perversions as a result of a perverse/incestuous relationship with their mothers.

Such is the case of Miss E, who was sent to me for consultation because of her compulsion to expose herself sexually to figures of authority, particularly women. This had led to her being expelled from everywhere; schools, training centres, jobs, counselling groups, and even mental hospitals, such was the havoc, puzzlement, and sense of impotence she had created in everyone.

She was a thirty-four-year-old plump, rather plain looking woman. When I first saw her she appeared to be eager to please and very scared. She gave me this impression despite the fact that I had been previously warned of her "dangerousness", meaning her tendency to develop crushes on women in authority and to make an absolute nuisance of herself to the point of pestering previous doctors with letters and phone calls and even unexpectedly showing up at their home addresses and pursuing them with her exhibitionistic behaviour.

She told me that her compulsion to "flash" occurred when she became attached to a person whom she invested with idealized "maternal" qualities. She wanted to get closer, to be noticed and to be taken care of by that particular person, but she also wanted a shocked response from her "victims". She carefully planned the "appropriate" gear to wear when she was to meet that person. Usually she wore an overcoat covering only a little vest in order to respond readily to her urges. She knew this was wrong and that she would be rejected but could not stop herself. She had had this urge since she was very small, but at first was able to contain it. At school she had a crush on one of her female teachers but limited her actions to undressing in her presence. This gave her much sexual pleasure. At the age of seventeen, while being trained in an institution, she developed another crush on the head person and for the first time succumbed to her compulsion. Since then she had been unable to bear the tension and had repeated the same action over and over again, with teachers, heads of institutions, doctors, bosses, etc. Each time this brought disaster. She was expelled from everywhere because of her "antisocial" behaviour, even by psychiatrists and psychotherapists who could not tolerate it.

On one occasion a victim of hers, an older woman, got furious and slapped her. She was surprised at her own reaction of intense enjoyment and sexual frenzy. She then instantly "learnt" that what she most wanted from these "mother figures" was to be either masturbated or slapped on the bottom by them. The referral letter stated that her actions seemed to be responding to masochistic needs rather than sexual relationships. She had never had a close relationship, emotionally or physically, with either sex. She had lived in institutions from the age of eight as pupil, trainee, employee, or in-patient.

It was not difficult to believe her own account of being masturbated by her mother from a very early age every time she felt sad or upset or to make her go to sleep, and her account was confirmed when mother was interviewed. Not only had she masturbated this little girl but also the other four children. In the mother's own words; "it was easier than to use a dummy". She said that at the time she felt depressed, had an unhappy marriage to a man who used to get drunk and beat her up constantly. She also admitted that these actions with her children gave her an enormous sense of comfort and elation. It was also her only way to make herself go to sleep.

My patient, like all perverse patients, had used splitting, projective identification, and sexualization as a survival kit in dealing with the outside world. She was employing manic defences in an attempt to deal with her intense, chronic, masked depression which resulted from a very deprived childhood, in which she was made to feel a part or continuation of her mother's body, only existing to provide her mother with narcissistic and sexual gratification. She was literally "something" located between her thighs that mother could touch, caress, or rub; whenever the patient felt like crying that was the only way to pacify her. She responded to this repetitive, incessant, and restless motion. She was nothing else, that was all. And in this she was not on her own; she had siblings who simultaneously had the same experience. She learnt that her way of survival was communal living where the law lay with the head person and independence or self-assertion were not permitted, while making as little trouble as possible amongst her peer group. The next move in her strategy was to develop a crush on the female head person who like mother would then use her. She was giving herself as a sacrificial victim in order to keep all of them together in harmony.

Her expectations for a shocked response in her victims had to do with a hopeful outcome in which women in authority—symbolic mothers—would not respond like her own mother, using and exploiting her as a part-object, but she had to test them to the extreme. By her pestering them through letters, phone calls, and visits to their "private" homes, she was in deep projective identification with her own mother's intrusiveness into her own "private" parts. She felt justified in so doing, since this had been done to her. She had now become the aggressor, she even saw herself as such by her own admission that what she was doing was wrong, though she could not help doing it.

So, as usual, behind her perverse actions lay the hope of a magic, hopeful outcome. She hoped to escape from her traumatic experiences as a child, yet her actions were imbued with such perverse psychopathology borrowed from her mother that she also sought total revenge. No emotional relationships had ever populated her inner world.

It is interesting to note that, even when her exhibitionism could superficially appear to be the equivalent of her male counterpart's, this is not so. It is a well-known fact that male exhibitionists have the compulsion to "flash" only to women—and to women who are unknown to them—while my patient had suffered from this compulsion only with other women whom she felt to be in close attachment. This is yet another remarkable difference between the genders.

Transference and countertransference

Workers of all disciplines involved in cases of incest frequently find it difficult to maintain a detached professional stance. They tend to take sides, usually becoming emotionally bound to the victims. Additionally, or alternatively, they feel punitive towards the perpetrators. In their distress, they lose their understanding of the dynamics of what is happening.

At other times professionals become so indignant that they fail to see that victims who become perpetrators experience a conscious or unconscious desire to take revenge for the pain inflicted upon them. These victims–perpetrators believe they are creating a situation in which justice is satisfied. Actually, however, they are identifying with their aggressors. In somewhat similar ways, the professional workers often identify with the victims. Supervision has an important role in clarifying these issues, thus enabling therapists to avoid such pitfalls.

Assessments of victim and victimizer patients can easily trigger off emotional responses in the professionals that may interfere with clear and unbiased treatment recommendations and are at times a re-enactment of early family situations.

The victims may succeed in making the therapist feel not only protective but also possessive about them, which could lead to patients feeling favoured and unique in individual treatment.

When dealing with the perpetrators, the therapist may feel cornered or blackmailed by confidentiality issues which may provoke feelings of collusion. Alternatively, the therapist might feel either like the consenting child or the seductive parent in the incest situation. Either way, dynamic therapy—meaning internal change—is in real jeopardy.

Group therapy for victims and perpetrators of incest

Group analytical psychotherapy can become, if well administered, the best form of treatment for victims and perpetrators of incest since they share, by nature of their predicament, a history of an engulfing, intense, inappropriate, distorted, physical, and sexual relationship of a highly secretive type within the family situation. Patients' psychopathologies are the product of severe traumas and early learnt survival mechanisms. Group analytical therapy breaks through patterns of self-deception, fraud, secrecy, and collusion that are invariably present in these cases. The group offers a family–social microcosm where every member knows about the secret, it allows for a new transferential–countertransferential process to take place for patients who present problems related to violence and secrecy in the family. Exclusive reliance on the therapist (parental figure), which takes place in a one-to-one therapy is discouraged, and trust towards peer members (sibling figures) is facilitated. This is specifically important since as children they felt completely isolated from their siblings. In this way group members open up and overcome the taboo of secrecy.

Group treatment of both victims and perpetrators of incest together but not related, offers unexpected qualities of containment and insight which are virtually impossible in a one-to-one situation (Welldon, 1997). Perpetrators become deeply aware of the extensive long term consequences of their actions. When confronted by the other members mirroring their victims' predicaments, it provides an opportunity for reflection, so that they can see how they experience themselves only *as parts of their parental figures* and are unable to see themselves as separate human beings. Every member experiences a powerful sense of belonging to the group. Throughout treatment patients gain a capacity for self-assertion, emotional growth, independence, and individuation. They see themselves and others developing into respected individuals with self-esteem that is acknowledged by others and by themselves. They are not only allowed but encouraged openly to express anger and frustration that has been kept hidden for lengthy periods. This encouragement comes especially from other old members who have gone through similar predicaments and who are now ready to leave.

I shall try to convey some of the transferential and countertransferential dilemmas encountered during the assessment process and later on during group analytical therapy with two of my patients who remained in therapy for many years and were able to make great therapeutic progress through fundamental inner changes. They are Kevin and Patricia, already mentioned earlier, the first a male perpetrator and the latter an incest victim.

Keith was referred for treatment after the disclosure of his incestuous relationship with his stepdaughter. I saw him for several diagnostic interviews. These were beset with complications as all the different agencies involved demanded information about his activities. I was placed in a double-bind situation, first because of his demands for immediate treatment and second because of his request for complete confidentiality. I began to feel cornered and blackmailed into giving him treatment in the utmost confidentiality that actually in this particular case meant secrecy. I became deeply aware of the transference–countertransference issues involved in "incest with a consenting child". These were very powerful feelings. At times I would feel like the child keeping quiet about it all; at other times, I would feel like the controlling and exploitative parental figure. After a great deal of careful thought I decided to offer him group therapy, a suggestion that first surprised and then enraged him. I gave him time to think about it, and tried to explain to him clearly why this would be the most suitable therapy for him: secrecy between parent and child is a key pathological trait in incest, which in group therapy becomes no longer available. Everything is open to everyone. A few weeks later it was my turn to be surprised when he accepted my recommendation.

During the assessment period with Patricia I felt protective of her, being an incest victim, and had the idea that the only person capable of fully understanding her was myself. At that point, I became aware of alarm bells ringing, which indicated that my initial response was in itself a contra-indication for offering individual therapy. I had already fallen for a complementary countertransferential response as an incestuous "parental" figure. When I offered her group therapy, she was terrified at the prospect of having to confront and be confronted by so many strangers, representing her own siblings, and at the idea of sharing her secret, but was able to understand the reasons for this recommendation.

It is not uncommon to observe that soon after entry to the group female patients with a history of early incest may behave in the group as pseudo ideal assistants to the therapist. Even those who have never been familiar with unconscious processes seem to discover immediately pseudo appropriate ways to "help" the therapist–mother–father keep the group–family together. This is exactly what happened when Patricia joined the group; she started behaving as the "ideal" assistant to the therapist, even though she had never previously been in any kind of psychotherapeutic treatment. She fulfilled perfectly the role of the incest victim who tries to keep the family together. Fellow patients often react with surprise and bewilderment at this show of false maturity. Later on this is replaced with competitiveness. When interpretations are made to the effect that the newcomer is only repeating a pathological pattern learnt early in life, other fellow patients seem relieved by this understanding, but it is then the turn of the patient pseudo helper to be filled with rage at this interpretation. After all, she is "doing her best"; why is she being so "harshly criticized"? Our group therapy programme treatment has provided new understanding of the complexities of abuse; through we are still far from understanding everything. In such mixed groups male perpetrators become aware that their actions are not just limited to temporary or transient physical effects but also inflict deep psychological wounds on their victims.

A few months after starting group treatment Patricia was in tears, telling us of her extreme humiliation on a recent visit to her parents, who, despite knowing that she was a vegetarian, confronted her on Saturday morning with an enormous breakfast of sausages and bacon, especially cooked by her father, which she reluctantly but acquiescently ate.

Whereas previously Keith and Patricia had been unable to make any connection, even refusing eye contact, they were now in open confrontation with one another. Keith became suddenly aware of the long-term consequences of the incest when he indignantly questioned her inability to assert herself and her compulsion to give in to her father's requests. Suddenly and quite unexpectedly a complete understanding of their own respective roles and of the implications was available to us all. We all became aware that incest is much larger than life, that its power is not only physical, sexual, or erotic. This secret union provides both partners with a "uniqueness" that is almost impossible to describe. It gives as much as it takes away.

It is also clear that victims, who may at the start be quiet and compliant, have much anger to express, anger that they have never felt free to display before. This is fundamental for them in being able to achieve any real change. It is essential to make an important difference between *anger*, expressed in a straightforward manner leading to self-assertion, and the harbouring of *revenge*, revealing the passion still existent in the victim intertwined with the original victimizer. At times, the victim claims she can now express anger against the perpetrator, but when this is in a twisted and vengeful way it is clear that she is still a partner in the old incestuous process.

In the group treatment Patricia began to assert herself slowly and in a determined fashion, but only after an initial period of being extremely compliant to the therapist in order to keep the "family" together. Eventually, she began to express anger, when she was able to scream at another group member and tell him to "sod off". She and everyone else were extremely surprised at this and we all experienced a sense of achievement at her newly gained ability to express anger.

However, our reaction was completely different when a few months later we saw her looking extremely elated, radiating a sense of triumph. Although everyone was aware of her mood as soon as she entered the room, nobody felt at ease with this feeling and somebody asked the reason for her feeling so triumphant. Her answer was, "The bastard got what he deserved." At that point everybody knew who she was talking about but nobody knew what she was referring to. Then she said, "The bloody bastard just got to know that his testicles will be removed because of cancer. Isn't that wonderful?"

A few members attempted a smile but most people felt extremely worried about her. I offered her an interpretation dealing with her inability to separate herself from her father in her strong need for revenge. We all know that the expression of anger is therapeutic and a healthy sign, but the wish for revenge is an unhealthy trait that poisons the person who suffers from it and everybody around her, too. This situation revealed how much the victims cling to the perpetrators like a necessary enemy.

Perpetrators initially display defensive mechanisms such as denial and avoidance. But later on, with the tolerance and acceptance of other fellow members, are able, perhaps for the first time, to look at themselves as abusers in a different light. This can only happen when understanding, not blame, is the aim. In his identification with the impotent and helpless victim the perpetrator gets angry on her behalf and demands that she be self-assertive and able to sever herself from her own abusers. In this way, incest victims gain recognition of their own "erotization of cruelty" (Milton, 1996) and are able to look at problems they are most ashamed of and in need of help with, including the addiction to the abuse and the abuser (van der Kolk, 1989). Artificial idealization of the victim status is no longer necessary.

The patients are fearful that the therapist, in a one-to-one situation, will lose control, and will fall prey to the patient's seduction, the outcome of which is both hoped for and dreaded. Their underlying anxiety is associated with tremendous fears of separation and being discarded by parental figures if they do not comply with their inappropriate demands. In group therapy they are confronted with reality testing from their co-equals, in which the power of being so favoured and unique (Ganzarain & Buchele, 1993) has to be worked through in the group situation, a bit like the family, though it operates on very different dynamics. Bentovim (1976, 1991, 1995) has produced extensive and invaluable studies that have highlighted the importance of the family dysfunction in the understanding, treatment, and management of the families with histories of incest.

In the course of group-analytical psychotherapy of a group composed of women and men, both genders containing perpetrators and victims of incest, patients' psychopathology involves shame, manic defences, and primitive defensive mechanisms such as denial, projection, and splitting. This tends to divide the helping professions; taking sides for either child or perpetrator and making them forget the neutral stance necessary to understand the whole family dynamics. In group therapy they are confronted with reality testing from their co-equals, and the position of being so favoured and unique has to be worked through in a group situation, a bit like the family, through it operates on very different dynamics. There is a generation gap in their real and emotional lives in which role reversal has occurred and the group interaction offers a completely different experience.

Group analysis offers a strict sense of boundaries with awareness of links between acts and unconscious motivations. The interpretation of vertical transference of the group in relation to the therapist–parental figures—usually with regressive elements—facilitates independence. Horizontal interpretations to do with mixed feelings about peer groups (sibling figures) provide the needed capacity to empathize with others, who actually represent parts of themselves. These are multiple transference processes, which are effectively used for the working through. These are not to be thought of as diluted, since they lead to heightened degrees of awareness.

Patients become aware in confrontation with their opposites of important dynamic processes involved, especially those related to their inability to think and their identification with the aggressor who was actually present in their early lives. Patients become aware of the reasons for their lack of trust and their intense need to be in control of all situations.

Slow-open groups offer different developmental stages from dependency to self-assertion, giving opportunities for senior members to take more caring roles, confronting junior members in therapeutic ways. It also provides evidence of emotional growth, which is acknowledged by other members and by the therapist facilitating individuation–separation never allowed by uncaring, neglectful parents and never observed in individual therapy. Time is the key to open the most primitive defence mechanisms, and "short, sharp, shock" treatment of such complex patients is doomed to failure.

I hope I have been able to convey that group psychotherapy offers particular advantages as a treatment option for victims of sexual abuse, since secrecy and isolation are replaced by disclosure within the containing atmosphere of the group. The threat of intimacy and the fantasized risks of seduction/exploitation are reduced for both patient and therapist. The power of the group as a whole acts both as an auxiliary ego in strengthening individuals as they confront past pain and abuse, and as a moderator of the sadistic need for revenge that fuels their innate capacity for perpetrating abuse in their turn, thus making it possible to break the cycle.

CHAPTER FIVE

Incest: the damaged psychic flesh

Mariam Alizade

Incests—in the plural

This paper, prompted by the Ravello conference on "Incest yesterday and today", deals with the different forms that incest can take, their fantasy representations, traumatic potential and dimensions of horror and desire.

In the eighth century BCE, Hesiod's *Theogony* describes Uranus (the sky) as the son of Gaia (the Earth), only to have him, a few lines later, father her children. The Earth becomes the wife of her own son. An incest of mythical origin, this is one example among many of the recurrence, throughout the centuries, of incestuous drives in the collective imagination of human beings.

Incest lies inside each of us as a fantasy, as indirect incest, and shapes us as powerfully as the prohibition against it is strong. The taboo is highly significant, in the sense that it becomes a fundamental regulatory force in human existence, even though the reason for so much horror or for such frequent transgression of the prohibition may not always be understood. The very fact of transgression shows how, for some people, incest is not a source of taboo or horror but of desire, upon which they act without any thought for the psychic consequences to the person whom they draw into forbidden intercourse.

The fact that it is more or less invariable as a universal prohibition does not imply that there are no different configurations; incest is a topic that has been studied by several disciplines. To actual incest, performed on the body, whether with full completion of the sexual act or with sexual commerce without actual penetration of the erogenous zones, more subtle forms of incest must be added such as verbal incest and incestuous stimulation. A psychoanalytical classification of the kinds of incest should also include such patterns as sublimated incest and consented incest.

Lévi-Strauss (1969), defining the taboo of incest as a cultural fact that applies to blood relations, highlights the transition from nature to culture. The sexual instinct is a major feature through which nature manifests itself, which is why the transition from one structural order to the other occurs in that domain rather than in any other. For Lévi-Strauss, the incest taboo is a rule that within a given society encompasses all that is most alien to it; at the same time, it is a social rule that keeps in check what in our nature seeks to disrupt it. The prohibition of incest is thus simultaneously on the threshold of culture and within culture; in a way, it is culture itself. Héritier-Augé (2001) introduces a greater complexity with her notion of incest of the second type, one which relates to the senses, where the prohibition lies in the fact of sharing the same sexual fluids or substances. Noting that the first type of incest, that between blood relations, involves the coming together of two bodies, she adds that two identical bodily substances may come into mutual contact without there being any direct physical contact—for example, when two relatives share the same sexual partner, there is a transfer of bodily fluids akin to what occurs in "fluid mechanics". This is the second type of incest, in which flesh and fluids come into contact via bodily "humours", and in particular those that in some civilizations are indeed called the "fluids of sex", masculine and feminine. The prohibitions apply to indirect incestuous contacts such as the relationship of a daughter and a mother with the same man, or the taboo that exists in some cultures against having intercourse with one's wife's sister. The taboo of incest is expressed through the transmission, contact and exchange of sexual fluids.

Freud studied the horror that incest evokes with reference to totemism (Freud. 1912–1913). He emphasized also that prohibitions do not depend on biological consanguinity but on the totemic kinship of certain tribal groups. Consanguinity is displaced on to the symbolic blood common to all clan members, and its structural effects on culture and social links are the same as in the case of the taboo involving direct consanguinity.

Clinical observations of actual cases of incest (Rascovsky & Rascovsky. 1950; Shengold, 1980) bring the psychoanalyst up against the surprising idea that some acts of incest may have unusual effects. Rascovsky and Rascovsky report a case of father–daughter incest. The patient, possibly severely borderline, manifested intense sadistic tendencies and promiscuous behaviour. The authors write:

> A study of this case enabled us to unify conclusions drawn from the observation of similar cases. We believe that the actual consummation of the incestuous relation, which constitutes a secondary process derived from a former grave state of melancholy, diminishes the subject's chance of psychosis and allows better adjustment to the external world. [Raskovsky & Rascovsky, 1950, p. 45]

Along the same lines, Shengold describes a case of consummated mother–son incest:

> Also this man who had been raised to look like a girl had perhaps been saved from homosexuality or at least some grave deformation of his sexual life by the incest. My last mystery: the incest consummated in adolescence appears to have undone some damage from early childhood. [Shengold, 1980, p. 473]

Later, he adds that the patient interrupted analysis, not having worked through the terror caused by the incestuos act.

These reported cases deserve to be carefully examined before accepting that any kind of benefit could arise from the perpetration of incest.

In any case, we must pay close attention to the many psychic effects and to the weight of culture, traditions, and habits on the mind at different periods of history.

It is impossible to make a purely general assessment of the overwhelming trauma that incest brings about. The complemental

series, the metapsychology of trauma, the quality of intersubjectiv-
ity, and the particularities of each case will make the experience
more or less pathogenic, depending on one or several of those
factors.

To my mind, the cultural impact of incest lies in the placing of
the word "No" (with a capital letter) as a determining factor in the
society's ethical code. This "No" (or veto) is initially manifested at
the very heart of sexuality in human beings, in their primary drives
and desires. The "No" of incest is a "No" that regulates interactions,
bringing into focus (through upbringing and the Superego) the
notion of "do Not touch", moral imperatives ("do Not steal," "do
Not kill," "do Not eat your fellow man", among others) and the
acceptance of limits and finitude. The series of "No" establishes
healthy forms of repression, which are necessary to bring about a
dissociation or split between neurotic and psychotic aspects (Bleger,
1967) of the personality, as well as the resulting development and
operation of the ego's discriminatory and selective functions (*ibid.*,
87ff.). This "No" applied to the drive-impelled desires with respect
to the primary objects is the first move towards taming the instinct
(Freud, 1937c, p. 225) by means of which the mind learns to surrender, to mediate, to wait, and to tolerate frustration.

This "do Not touch" arising from psychosexuality has to
combine with its instinctual counterpart "not to be sexually touched
by the incestuous object": to respect this "No" requires that both
participants in the prohibition observe the taboo. It is a constructive
"No" that permeates the family structure, ruling its functions and
operating as a law. The horror of incest is linked to the threat of
death (transgression of taboo and punishment), to the fear of castration, to being thrown out of the symbolic order of things. This horror
inhibits the desire that tends towards the incestuous act.

Throughout his work, Freud quite rightly gave psychosexuality
a major role in all human development; in this particular domain,
its sheer force is unmistakable.

Incestuous fantasies

Incestuous contact, in terms of a libidinal bond and desire-driven
penetration between two blood relatives, is an experience that all

human beings have at the moment of their birth. Two blood relatives are libidinously united in a profoundly intimate relationship. The state of merging or fusion between mother and son is unavoidably incestuous (Green, 2001) and implies the inevitability of this kind of incestuous contact as a requirement for life. Incest serves as an introduction to instinct, as a magical testimony to an inaugural love relationship in which everything is permitted within the framework of this desired interaction. This kind of orgasm, as Freud (1905d, p. 180) described the feeling of satiation immediately after the infant has suckled, constitutes the first sign of incestuous eroticism.[1] The absence of incest in *this* sense of maximum desire and intercourse with a primary object would constitute a far greater tragedy. This kind of incestuous bond is usually accompanied by an ethical intention by the significant adult towards the new-born child and the respect for the prohibition. The taboo itself is observed; there is maximum closeness, but the dividing barrier, established by culture, is maintained. In one session, a young mother reported a dream that had been triggered by her new-born baby crying during the night before she rose to feed him: "My baby is lying on top of me, we move rhythmically, everything is peaceful and very pleasant, as if we were having sex." The patient woke up, attended to her son and, a few hours later, as she lay on the analytical couch, she reported her dream with a mixture of surprise and delight. The dream shows the persistence of non-traumatic, unconscious incestuous impulses and the fact that they may lead to happy and contented mothering.

At an intra-psychic level, incestuous desires and fantasies participate in the primal fantasy of going back inside the maternal womb; they lie concealed in pre-oedipal anxiety and come vividly back to life in the oedipal period, when the instinctual desires have as their aim the objects that are forbidden by the taboo of incest. The desire for the "forbidden other" generates tension and conflict, the resolution of which demands working-through in the mind and causes inevitable mental pain arising from the experience of these primary tragedies of deep love and hate.

The child learns to apply the "No" to the power of his or her instinctual drives. As I have already stated, cultivating this "No" in the framework of biological immaturity leads to the child's first steps towards taming the instincts. The prohibition imperative,

with its roots somewhere between nature and culture, has a civilizing influence on the child and lends structure to the path that leads
to adulthood. The wild horse of primitive passion is tamed through
subsequent acts of relinquishment, thanks to which the intense
cathexis of the first objects fades. The "No"—and this is an issue I
would like to insist on—is mutual, reciprocal, since the adults who
belong to the forbidden circle must also re-educate their own incestuous instincts, always present to some extent even if in a sublimated and partly repressed way.

If we observe what happens within the marital couple, the
fantasy of incest, on certain occasions, takes on a pathogenic character, to such an extent that it may render the husband impotent
(Freud, 1912d) if he projects incestuous fantasies on to his erotic
object. If the wife is in fantasy equated with the mother, the prohibition will fall on her, thus impoverishing and creating a split in
erotic life.

The same incestuous fantasy may, however, have the opposite
effect, and become a beneficial incestuous intention. As Freud wrote
(1912d, p. 186):

> It sounds not only disagreeable but also paradoxical, yet it must
> nevertheless be said that anyone who is to be really free and happy
> in love must have surmounted his respect for women and have
> come to terms with the idea of incest with his mother or sister.

The fellow being, the one chosen by the laws of exogamy, is a recip-
ient of part of the incestuous fantasy. This imaginary transgression
opens up a whole universe of delight for the erogenous flesh when
an illusory fusion with the other person takes place, the person of
primal love, the primitive, dreamed-of father, mother, or sibling.
Exogamy and endogamy become united in a common path.

Obnoxious incest

I would divide incest into two classes: asymmetrical or intergenerational incest (father–child, grandfather–grandchild, etc.) and
symmetrical (sibling incest). The kind of incest that I call asymmetrical is characterized by two elements: one is the generation gap
between the two participants in the incestuous scenario, the other

is the exercise of power by one of them in order to force the other person into submission. This would also be the case, for example, where a slightly older sibling may make an incestuous invitation to forbidden games that leave a mark on the psyche as revealed in subsequent deferred actions. Sibling incest may become asymmetrical in so far as it may not have been freely consented to, or it may occur in a symmetrical situation of interchange between peers (sibling incest proper).

The use of the "other"—baby, child, adolescent—and the exercise of power over the weaker person are tendencies that contribute to the physical incestuous act. In asymmetrical incest, a body is subjected to sexual harassment and intruded upon by the sexual endogamic act of an important family member. The mother or father makes intrusive and forbidden contact with the body of a child. The young flesh suffers the trauma of an adult invasion. This act awakens feelings of fear and conflicts of emotions involving love and hate.

In every case, the act is literally "a family affair".

In what I call the obnoxious type of incest, the more vulnerable participant, whose consent has at most been minimal, experiences the pleasant effects of seduction together with subsequent confusion. He or she may have been tempted by the promise of stepping into the place of a chosen child (or grandchild), maybe even becoming the favourite, the most suitable one for the love that the adult hints at, either overtly or not, through his or her sexually-stimulating approach. Clinical practice has shown us how this pleasure later turns into a source of guilt and the need for atonement, how it has been a kind of lure to obtain the consent of the child or adolescent. This point is worth emphasizing: there is always some degree, albeit minimal, of consent or at least passivity. The rebelliousness or the shouting that would have hindered or interrupted the scene are quelled; they will be expressed years later, when the story is reconstructed on the analytical couch or when psychotherapy manages to make its way into the associative complex of life experience and open up the memories of the incestuous event. Obedience, submission, and hapless complicity are partly explained on the basis of surprise, fear of the supremacy of the invading adult on whom the youngster depends and whom in some way he or she loves, and the uncertain and paralysing feeling that some act is occurring that is at once immensely transcendent and infinitely forbidden. An act that we may call extreme when it occurs between two bodies that belong to the same family, bodies that had up till then kept their distance, when one person violates a rule sacred in nature; both participants coalesce together in the mutual exploration of the most intimate of their body areas, exchanging their fluids, in a manner that is forbidden and punished by the ethical code of the culture.

At a particular moment in time the familiar family member suddenly takes on a new, strange, almost unrecognizable role, that of child seducer. A close male relative, for example, penetrates the forbidden body of the child. Asymmetry here is not only mental but also physical because the young person's body is not yet genitally mature and will therefore be hurt and torn. Incest makes this event happen earlier than it should, thus paying no heed to the child's latency.

Through a kind of manipulation disguised as game playing, the perpetrator can often accelerate the natural course of events regarding erogenous arousal. This deliberate acceleration of arousal, much earlier than the child's natural time-frame would allow, is clearly violent. The other person, the child, is used and possessed, with neither regard nor respect for his or her autonomy and individuality.

The child is treated as a thing; the parent projects on to and into the young person his or her own hate, guilt feelings, and deepest conflicts.

The traditional role of parenting—balanced education, developing maturity, responsible attitude—is brutally replaced by dismantling, perversity, and pathological bonds.

If we take Gadamer´s view (1993. p. 88) that body and life are as one, incest automatically becomes a crime. The defiled body is haunted forever by a dark cloud. The burden of incest interrupts harmonious development and condemns the victims to live with this past trauma always present. The child or adolescent is engulfed by feelings of confusion and humiliation. They have to dissociate themselves from their own being, their own *Eigenheit* ("self-ownership"). Their private space has been broken into, their inner silence deafened by the ongoing act.

The function of the family and the adult parenting role that both mother and father should be guaranteeing fade into the background. The true family role of the parents is no longer fulfilled.

The silent parent—the one who does not actually commit the act—often turns a blind eye to the events and in so doing is just as much of an accomplice. What children have to say is often discredited by their parents, so that they feel obliged to remain silent. If they do not it may result in further mistreatment. Their guilt, shame and fear are shut up inside. During a session a girl said to me: "What I can't stand is that my mother won't believe me and insists that I am telling lies."

Disbelief of this sort and its accompanying secrecy build up into even greater suffering, becoming an extra layer of pain. The young person experiences a state of helplessness and confusion, self-inflicted contempt, guilt due to the pleasure that the seduction may have provoked, shame in front of his or her peer group, hatred for the failure to understand what is going on.

As Ferenczi (1933, p. 228) put it: "When the child recovers from such an attack, he feels enormously confused, in fact split—innocent and culpable at the same time—and his confidence in the testimony of his own senses is broken."

The main psychic consequences

First, damage to the symbolic function isolates the young person from culture; such youngsters feel themselves to be segregated and they know from the outset that an act of this kind must remain secret—one that carries the weight of a condemnatory sentence. It cannot be verbalized or shared, either within the family circle or in the wider world outside of the family; it becomes a secret, shameful stigma. Having forbidden sex and not saying anything is the formula that typifies the transgression of the incest taboo. To pleasure, when there is some, should be added a tragic dimension. The sharing of bodily flesh within the family gives the child victims an evil kind of pleasure, which they cannot or do not know how to avoid, and which forces them to keep to themselves a shameful secret that haunts and takes over their mind. The sombre awareness of a shared crime stimulates unconscious feelings of guilt and what Rosenberg (1991) calls *deadly* masochism, in the sense that it is indisputably linked to the death drive. The young people involved have been completely destroyed as regards the intimacy of their *soma*; they were not consulted, they were not respected as to their otherness. The act occurred without asking their permission, by means of an abuse of authority and the use of the young person's physical and emotional dependence on the adult. Helplessness, rape and silence make up a frequent pathogenic triad. The notion of sacrifice is close: the adult uses the young person's psychic flesh as if it were his or her own to possess, indifferent to the subsequent effect on the victim. The perpetrator's taking over their mind interferes with learning processes, and undermines the joy of living. Associative circuits are impaired, and anxiety and dissatisfaction increase. Both mind and body have been assaulted, since this is also an attack on thinking, a distortion of reality, and a confusion in the understanding of what it means to be a human being.

An extended incestuous experience disturbs the latency period, and causes pathological arousal at the wrong time, thereby damaging the growth process, the richness of identity consolidation, learning and development.

The situation of violence and confusion demands that the mind set up inflexible defence mechanisms such as disavowal and splitting. These in turn drain off all vital energy and lead to mental stagnation. The fact that resolution of the Oedipus complex is consequently impossible means that many patients are overwhelmed by conflictual networks of love and hate, crime and punishment, in a sort of endless pathological spiral that constitutes a barrier to the successful negotiation of the oedipal situation.

A patient who had been exposed to constant verbal incest throughout her childhood and adolescence said on several occasions in the course of her sessions: "My head seemed to explode, I had those thoughts inside myself and could not stop thinking about my father's words, about his dreams of incest that he told me of in detail, and about my own dreams; at times I wanted to die, I just could not stand it any more . . ."

In the analytical process: observation of Nathalie

Within the framework of psychoanalysis and psychoanalytic therapy, incest in its dimension as a real event manifests itself in the retelling as an experience anchored in time; in addition, it takes on the status of a psychic event, thereby allowing us to observe its effects and influence throughout life.

Some psychoanalytic observations in clinical studies with young victims of asymmetrical incest brought up in institutions have highlighted the following outcomes:

1. Identification with the aggressor, from victim to perpetrator. Uncontrollable promiscuity, disorganization of instinctual drives, drug addiction, psychopathic tendencies, lack of commitment, and emotional disorders are some of the major trends that have been observed.
2. Reparation, sublimation, protective a-sexuality. Nathalie, a patient that I will introduce in the final part of this paper, said when speaking of her plans for the future: "When I grow up, I want to become a kindergarten teacher and take care of children."
3. Severe mental illness: psychosis (Quallenberg, 2002).
4. Somatic illness.

Sometimes during the session the analyst becomes the comforter and organizer of the young person's mind. The transference process is a kind of mental nourishment for the young incest victim. At other times, in fantasy, the patient can re-experience in the transference the traumatic neurosis and perceive the analyst at this point of the therapy as a possible perpetrator.

Through deferred actions, the incestuous scenario will be expressed in different fantasies during the working-through process.

Indignation is often felt by the analyst who has to face this all-too-familiar horror.[2]

The analyst tries to draw the patient back into the circle of humanity, to repair the body as it is experienced in the patient's own mind, and to establish a new equilibrium.

The analyst, within the positive transference, acts as a restorer of law, desegregates the patient, and helps to reorganize the victim's symbolic universe. The secret is brought into the open and explored in subsequent sessions, and the right to exogamy in the fullest sense of the word is not only made conscious but also reconquered as the treatment progresses. Words are put on the incestuous act in its traumatic aspect, and the pathogenic psychic consequences begin to wane. The patient, together with the analyst, experiences inevitable feelings of hatred, necessary for facilitating the processes of discrimination and for distancing the victim from the abuse suffered; there is also a reordering of the values that bring the victim back into the folds of society with the feeling of being fully entitled to exogamy. This is tantamount to rescuing him or her from the threat of distortion—or even catastrophe—at the level of self-identity.

I will conclude this paper with a short vignette of a polytrau-matized girl, a victim of incest, whose words will leave painful echoes in our ears (Alizade, 1995).[3]

> Nathalie is fourteen years old. Her mother was repeatedly beaten up by her father, a brutal and violent alcoholic. One day the mother left home.
>
> The father also beat up Nathalie: "He beat me with a stick, in the face, my nose bled". He also raped her many times, both vaginally and anally, causing damage to the girl's bladder. Because of the beatings on her face, Natalie lost an eye.
>
> She was forced to take part in sexual play between her father and step-mother. In desperation, she ran away to seek help. In the end, the police came and arrested the father. The police and the child-care authorities restored order. The consequences of the trauma she suffered have made Nathalie extremely defensive concerning everything that has to do with her body; but, very slowly and with considerable difficulty, she is beginning to overcome the horror to which she had been subjected in her family.
>
> The physical nightmares are over, but now she has to work through the nightmares that inhabit her mind.
>
> During one session, she told me:
>
> "He made me go to bed with my stepmother, she was afraid, then she pinched me to make me do it, otherwise he would beat us both, we kissed each other's tits, he made me say things to her, that I should let her suck me . . .. My stepmother sucked my tits and between my legs, my father put in his willy front and back, it hurt me, he punched and pulled my hair. I told him I was shitting myself, let me go . . . And she pinched me and hurt me, he hurt me in the back and I started to bleed, it was painful and it still hurts now when I go to the toilet."

Some time later, she said:

"My bones hurt, my left shoulder hurts, my throat hurts, I always get colds and when I cough my forehead hurts . . . When my stepmother made me wash the dishes it was too much, I felt weak, my whole arm aches now . . ."

Notes

1. According to Freud (1905d, p. 180), "Sensual sucking involves a complete absorption of attention and leads either to sleep or even to a motor reaction in the nature of an orgasm." He goes on: "No one who has seen a baby sinking back satiated from the breast and falling asleep with flushed cheeks and a blissful smile can escape the reflection that this picture persists as a prototype of the expression of sexual satisfaction in later life" (*ibid.*, p. 182).
2. S. Amati has described this indignation during work with political refugees who had been victims of crimes against humanity.
3. I have described this case in a previous book (Alizade, 1995) *Clínica con la Muerte* (Near death: clincial studies).

CHAPTER SIX

Counterpoints

Brendan MacCarthy

Incest and loss

Previous contributions, in their very rich presentations, make the link between incestuous acts and an experience of loss. In my work with incestuous families, this connection was apparent in several ways.

One was the part played by the father's "loss" of the victim (and we are mainly talking of father–daughter incest here) when the child leaves home to attend school, at the age of five or six years. This is a peak age for the onset of an incestuous relationship. A father I interviewed defended himself in this way: "She used to be my little girl, she loved her daddy, but now all she talks about is her favourite teacher. She has no time for me any more."

It is striking too, how frequently it is found that prior to the first encounter there has been a significant loss, such as a breakup with a partner or a major family bereavement, notably the death of the perpetrator's mother. It is as though the experience of such losses mobilizes a need to seek restitution by reasserting earlier rights to intimacy over the child, in an attempt to undo the loss.

If the incestuous act begins within the first five years, the victim seldom has a clear memory or any understanding of the event. The child may tolerate inappropriate contact because, not long before, parents were felt to have the right to touch, clean, and in general manage what are commonly called the child's "private parts".

Indeed, in the first two or three years, the child accepts genital and anal ministrations, as though these areas were the prerogative of the parents or carers. So, as the child takes over control of their own orifices (and it is a requirement for entry to most schools in the UK that the child should have attained sphincter mastery), an exploratory touching, especially, as often happens, at night when the child is sleepy or asleep is felt by the child like a "return of the repressed".

It is a common practice in families for a parent to "lift" a sleeping child for the purpose of urination, in order to reduce the chance of a wet bed. On this question of "whose body is it anyway?" the small child may not be at all clear.

So the assertion of parental authority over the child's body may, confusedly, seem like the expression of an ancient right. And if contact with semen is experienced, the young child may confuse that with *her* urinary incontinence. At that age, especially in a regressed state, there is sure to be a degree of zonal confusion and confusion between self and object.

Gender of the analyst

In the analytic encounter, the incest victim, whether or not the abuse has been declared to the analyst, will see echoes of her past in the analytic setting.

An arrangement that excludes the possibility of intruders, and, allied to this privacy an implicit or explicit guarantee of confidentiality, is sure to find resonances. Interpretations can be experienced as penetrations, and analytic silence can seem equivalent to maternal collusion. Indeed, free association, our "golden rule", can seem to invite any words or any actions, without fear of consequences. To some, who have been exploited in the past, all this may seem like an invitation for further exploitation. But these echoes, or "proximities", in time provide a sense of safety and security, because of the discovery that analytic intimacy does *not* lead to exploitation. One young woman said, after a very fearful onset in analysis, "it was only after I was coming to you for more than a year that I realized that it was not true, as my former feminist friends in an incest survivers group insisted, that all men are bastards."

One point that arises in all this is the question of the sex of the analyst.

It is a generally held view by analysts that the sex of the analyst is more or less irrelevant in most cases, but incest victims usually feel very strongly about analyst sex choice, many refusing to contemplate a male analyst, others preferring a male "since my problems stem from a relationship with a man, I can only work it out effectively with a man". I find it best to give the patient freedom of choice, but thereafter to explore in analysis the conscious and unconscious reasons for the choice they made.

Ethical boundaries

To take up another point, relating to ethical issues. I have carried out a thorough literature search, not only of the psychoanalytic literature, but also of mental health literature more widely, and of forensic and legal literature.

I have noted that boundary violations, especially of incest victims, are virtually not represented in more intensive therapies, particularly psychoanalysis, but are much commoner in once weekly therapies or less than once weekly treatments.

The object intermittently seen would seem to be more tantalizing to both parties, more dangerous liaisons; while those closer to full analysis, and where, crucially, for that reason, the transference is central to the work, do not usually lead to abusive situations. Of course there are so many variables that this subject would require more consideration than we have time for today, but on another occasion it would merit more examination, and it has rich research potential.

This issue of greater availability (rather than every session ending with the rejecting "I'll see you next week") is illuminated by the contribution of Monique Cournut-Janin, in which she describes the service provided by her institution in Paris, which is open twenty-four hours daily, and 365 days per year for crisis walk-in cases. There are not many cities with a service like that, and its relevance is apparent from the fact that the majority of acts of sexual abuse and violence occur at night.

Are there precursors of the incestuous act?

We all have our infantile sexuality inside us somewhere, and which, in certain circumstances, can be re-enacted. What I think is quite important is to reflect on the genesis of incestuousness, rather than concerting on locating the time and place of the "act". Does an act of incestuous union come "out of the blue", or are there precursors?

Is incest impulsive and opportunistic or calculated? Or is it both? Here are two contrasting illustrations. I interviewed a twenty-year-old law student, following a serious suicidal attempt. When he was four years old, he was very sick one night. His mother undressed him, and, in order to change all the bedclothes and pyjamas, put the naked boy in her place in her bed, with father. Father began to touch his body, especially his genitals and repeated this the following day. This gradually progressed to full mutual penetrative sex over the following years, and only came to an abrupt end at the time of the suicidal attempt, a few weeks before I saw him. He desperately wanted to know from me, "because you are an expert", he said sarcastically, whether, if he had not been sick that night, it would ever have happened? The unconscious meaning behind his question was his belief that what happened was his fault, and the suicidal attempt included an act of self punishment.

The second example seems to highlight a considerable degree of calculation unlike the previous more opportunistic example. In the mid 1980s I saw a family of two parents with identical twin fifteen-year-old daughters. I had seen the daughter who had been for years in an incestuous relationship with father the week previously, and I had set up a further family meeting. When I entered the waiting room, I saw the two girls dressed identically, and they were so totally identical that I was unsure which one I had seen the previous week! In a later interview with father, I became interested in why he chose one girl but not the other. To give his reply, I will give the girls fictitious names. He said, "That was not difficult. They may look alike, but they are very different in temperament. Angela has always been a secretive and very compliant child, and I knew I could trust her to keep a secret. Mary was a blabberer, she would have screamed blue murder, and would tell the whole world. I'd never have risked it with her."

This led me to explore where and when the incestuous impulse begins.

I began to ask offenders when they first had the idea of a sexual relationship with their daughter. Some answered that it was a spur of the moment impulse, thought up and enacted with little fore-thought, but some other answers were a big surprise. The first person I asked said "Day one". "What do you mean?" I asked. "In the hospital, the nurse came out and said 'Mr X, you have a lovely little daughter', and I felt a slight sexual arousal. I had produced my own female." This girl became his victim. Another patient said he felt sexually aroused in the middle of his wife's pregnancy when they were going through the names for a boy or a girl (in those days, they did not know the gender in advance). When talking of girl's names he felt sexually aroused.

There is a sense in which the patient who brings her incest history, especially to a male professional, is rather like the nurse who says "You've got a girl". The patient is watching your reaction very carefully to see whether you will look shocked, disapprove, become excited or even aroused.

One promiscuous teenager asked at a consultation, "Does my incest story turn you on?"

Incest: yesterday, today and tomorrow

I will finish by saying that Simona Argentieri's text is about "incest yesterday and today", but I believe that we might need to think about "incest tomorrow" as well, because we need to consider gathering material about completed treatments and follow-up outcome studies. We are living in an era when evidence-based medicine is demanded everywhere. We cannot just say that we take histories, and we talk about the Oedipus complex, but we don't know what happens, or whether our work leads to long-term benefit.

I believe that follow-up will show that for these cases psycho-analytic therapy is far superior to other approaches including medication. This is why I think that it is worthwhile to consider this book—and the Conference that inspired it—just as a first valuable contribution to promote further discussion and reflection. Initiatives of this sort would be a powerful source of enlightenment for those many collegues who are not afraid to face the analytic challenge these damaged patients confront us with.

I hope that in the near future we could think about "Incest: Yesterday, Today and Tomorrow", to enable us to monitor our work in progress.

References

Alizade, A. M. (1995). *Near Death: Clinical Studies*. Buenos Aires: Amorrortu editores.

Alvarez, A. (1992). *Live Company*. London Tavistock/Routledge.

Amati Mehler, J. (1992). Love and male impotence. *International Journal of Psycho-Analysis, 73*: 467–480.

Angot, C. (1999). *Incest*. Paris: Editions Stock.

Argentieri, S. (1982a). Sui processi mentali precoci dell'identità femminile. *Rivista di Psicoanalisi, XXVIII*(3): 361–376.

Argentieri, S. (1983) Recensione a : M. Krüll, *Padre e figlio. Vita Familiare di Freud. Rivista di Psicoanalisi, XXIX*(4): 585–590.

Argentieri, S. (1985). Sulla cosiddetta disidentificazione dalla madre. *Rivista di Psicoanalisi, XXXI*(3): 397–403.

Argentieri, S. (1988). Il sesso degli angeli. In: L. Russo & M. Vigneri (Eds.), *Del genere sessuale*. Rome: Borla.

Argentieri, S. (1993). More than one analyst in the family—Sigmund and Anna Freud. *International Psycho-Analytical Association Newsletter, 2*: 24–26.

Argentieri, S. (1999). *Il padre materno. Da San Giuseppe ai nuovi mammi*. Rome: Meltemi.

Baranes, J. J. (1995). Double narcissique et clivage du moi. In: *Monographies de la Revue Française de Psychanalyse: Le Double* (pp. 39–53). Paris: PUF (Presses Universitaires de France).

Bataille, G. (1957). L'énigme de l'inceste. In: *L'Érotisme*. Paris: Editions de Minuit. English edition: The enigma of incest. In: *Eroticism* (M. Dalwood, Trans.) (pp. 197–220). London: Marion Boyars (1962).

Bentovim, A. (1976). Shame and other anxieties associated with breast feeding: a systems theory and psychodynamic approach. In: *Breast Feeding and the Mother, Ciba Symposium 45* (pp. 159–178). Amsterdam: Elsevier.

Bentovim, A. (1991). Clinical work with families in which sexual abuse has occurred. In: C. R. Hollin & K. Howells (Eds.), *Clinical Approaches to Sex Offenders and Their Victims* (pp. 179–208). Chichester: Wiley.

Bentovim, A. (1995). *Trauma-organised Systems. Physical and Sexual Abuse in Families*. Revised edn. London: Karnac.

Bion, W. R. (1961). *Experiences in Groups*. London: Tavistock.

Bleger, J. (1967). Estudio de la parte psicótica de la personalidad. In: *Simbiosis y Ambigüedad*. Buenos Aires: Editorial Paidós. English edition: *Symbiosis and Ambiguity: The Psychoanalysis of Very Early Experience*. London: Process Press (1999).

Ceccarelli, F. (1978). *Il tabù dell'incesto*. Turin: Einaudi.

Ciba Foundation (1984). *Sexual Abuse within the Family*. London: Tavistock.

Cournut-Janin, M. (1998). *Féminin et féminité*. Paris: P.U.F.

Couvreur, C. (1995). Les motifs du double. In: *Monographies de la Revue Française de Psychanalyse: Le Double* (pp. 19–37). Paris: PUF.

De Lauro Poletti, L. (1990. L'affettività fraterna: una dimensione da esplorare. Convegno SPI di Saint Vincent, maggio.

De Marchi, F., Ellena, A., & Cattarinussi, B. (Eds.) (1987). *Nuovo Dizionario di Sociologia*. Milan: Edizioni paoline.

De Simone, G. (2002). *Le famiglie di Edipo*. Rome: Borla.

Demause L. (1992). The history of the child assault. *Bulletin of the British Psychoanalytic Society*.

Doi, T. (1971)[1991]. *Anatomia della dipendenza*. Milan: Raffaello Cortina Editore.

Donnet, J. L. (2002). Dalla regola fondamentale alla situazione analizzante. *Psicoanalisi*, 6(2).

Durkheim, E. (1895). *Les règles de la méthode sociologique*, vol 1, Paris.

Durkheim, E. (1898). La prohibition de l'inceste. *L'année sociologique*, 1:

Ellis, H. (1905). *Sexual Selection in Man*. Philadelphia: F. A. Davis.

Fain, M., & Braunschweig, D. (1975). *La nuit, le jour*. Paris: P.U.F.

Fornari, F., (1982). L'Edipo come preconcezione, *Gruppo e funzione analitica*, III(3): 27–39.

Fortune R. (1932). Voce "Incest", in *Encyclopedia of the Social Science.* New York.

Freud, S. (1887–1904). *The Complete Letters of Sigmund Freud to Wilhelm Fliess,* J. M. Masson (Ed.), Harvard University Press, 1985.

Freud, S. (1892–94). Preface and footnotes to the translation of Charcot's *Tuesday Lectures. S.E., 1.*

Freud, S. (1895d). Studies on hysteria. *S.E., 2.*

Freud, S. (1905d). Three essays on the theory of sexuality. *S.E., 7.*

Freud, S., (1910h). A special type of choice of object mode by men. *S.E., 11.*

Freud, S. (1912d). Contribution to the psychology of love, II. On the universal tendency to debasement in the sphere of love. *S.E., 11:* 179–190, London: Hogarth.

Freud, S. (1912–13). The horror of incest. In "Totem and taboo". *S.E., 13:* 1–17.

Freud, S. (1913–1914). Totem and taboo. *S.E., 13.*

Freud, S. (1914). On the history of the psycho-analytic movement. *S.E., 14.*

Freud, S. (1916–17). Introductory lectures on psycho-analysis. *S.E., 16.*

Freud, S. (1923b). The ego and the id. *S.E., 19.*

Freud, S. (1924d). The dissolution of the Oedipus complex. *S.E., 19:* 173–179. London: Hogarth.

Freud, S. (1931b). Female sexuality. *S.E., 21,* London: Hogarth.

Freud, S. (1937c). Analysis terminable and interminable. *S.E., 23.*

Freud, S. (1939a). Moses and monotheism. *S.E., 23.*

Gadamer, H. (1993)[2001]. Experiencia y Objetivización del cuerpo. In: *El estado oculto de la salud* (pp. 87–100). Barcelona: Gedisa Editorial.

Gaddini, E. (1984). Whether and how our patients have changed up to the present day. In: *Changes in Analysts and in Their Training.* IPA Monograph, Series 4.

Gallino, L. (1978). Voce "Sociologia della Famiglia". In: *Dizionario di Sociologia.* UTET.

Ganzarain, R., & Buchele, B. (1993) Group psychotherapy for adults with a history of incest. In: H. Kaplan & B. Sadock, (Eds), *Comprehensive Group Psychotherapy* (pp. 515–525). Baltimore, MD: Williams & Wilkins.

Giannakoulas, A. (2002). Uso e abuso del bambino attraverso i secoli, Convegno per il Decennale dell'A.I.Psi., 1992–2002. 16 November, Rome, Campidoglio, unpublished.

Godelier, M. (1996). *L'énigme du don*. Paris: Fayard. English edition: *The Enigma of the Gift*. (N. Scott, Trans.). Chicago: University of Chicago Press (1999).

Goethe, J. W. (1785–1907)[1979]. *La vocazione teatrale di Wilhelm Meister*. Milan: Mondadori.

Green, A. (1979). L'angoisse et le narcissisme. In: A. Green (Ed.) (1983), *Narcissisme de Vie, Narcissisme de Mort* (pp. 133–173). Paris, Minuit. *Life Narcissism, Death Narcissism*. (A. Weller, Trans.). New York: Free Association Books.

Green, A. (1992)[1994]. *Slegare*. Rome: Borla.

Green, A. (1993). Pulsion de mort, narcissisme négatif, fonction désobjectalisante. In: *Le Travail du Négatif*. Paris: Editions de Minuit. English edition (1999), *The Work of the Negative*. (A. Weller, Trans.). New York: Free Association Books.

Green, A. (2001). "La relation mère-enfant, nécessairement incestueuse". In *Incestes* (pp. 29–40). Paris: PUF.

Greenacre, P. (1967). L'influenza del traumma infantile sui modelli genetici. In: *Studi Psicoanalitici sullo sviluppo emozionale*. Florence: Martinelli, 1979. English edition: The influence of trauma on the genetic models. In: S. S. Furst (Ed.), *Psychic Trauma* (pp.108–153). New York: Basic Books.

Grimal, P. (1976). *Dictionnaire de la mythologie grecque et romaine*. Paris. PUF.

Grünberger, B. (1977)[1971]. *Il narcisismo*. Bari: Laterza.

Harris, M. (1968). *The Rise of Anthropological Theory. A History of Therories of Culture*. New York: Crowell.

Héritier-Augé, F. (1994). L'ordre caché des choses. In: O. Jacob (Ed.), *Les deux Soeurs et leur Mère*. Paris. English edition (1999): *Two Sisters and their Mother, the Anthropology of Incest*. (J. Herman, Trans.). New York: Zone Books; London: MIT Press (distributor).

Héritier-Augé, F. (2001). Inceste et substance. Oedipe, Allen, les autres et nous. In: *Incestes*. Paris: PUF.

Hobhouse, L. T., Wheeler G. C., & Ginsberg, M. (1915). *The Material Culture and Social Institution of the Simpler Peoples: an Essay in Correlation*. London: Chapman & Hall.

Laplanche, J. (1986). De la théorie de la séduction restreinte à la théorie de la séduction généralisée. *Etudes Freudiennes*, 27: 7–25.

Legendre, P. (1985) L'artifice juridique de la légitimité: l'objet interdit. In: L'inestimable objet de la transmission (pp. 69–85). Paris: Fayard.

Lévi-Strauss, C. (1947)[1965, 1969]. Le problème de l'inceste. In: *Les Structures Elementaires de la Parenté*. Paris. Mouton. English edition:

The problem of incest. In: J. R. von Sturmer & R. Needham (Eds.), *The Elementary Structures of Kinship* (J. H. Bell, Trans.), revised edition, 1969. Boston: Beacon Press.

Lowie, R. (1920). *Primitive Society.* New York: Boni & Liveright.

Mair, L., 1971, *Marriage.* Harmondsworth:

Malinowski, B. (1927). *Sex and Repression in Savage Society.* London:

Mancia, M. (1985). Recensione a "J. F. Masson: *Assalto alla verità*". *Rivista di Psicoanalisi, XXXI*(1): 131–139.

Marcuse, M. (1915). *Von Inzest.* Halle: Carl Markold.

Mauss, M. (1950). *Sociologie et anthropologie.* Paris: P.U.F.

MacCarthy, B. (1982a). Incest and psychotherapy. *Irish Journal of Psychotherapy, 1*: 11–16.

MacCarthy, B. (1982b). Incest, a fatal psychoanalytic illness? *Bulletin of the British Psychoanalytic Society.*

McDougall, J. (1995). *The Many Faces of Eros.* London: Free Association Books.

McLennan, J. F. (1865). *Primitive Marriage.* Edinburgh: A & C Black.

Menahem, R. (1995). Qui a peur de son double?. In: *Monographies de la Revue Française de Psychanalyse: Le Double* (pp. 119–134). Paris. PUF.

Milton, J. (1996). Technical problems in the psychotherapy of perverse female patients. In: E. V. Welldon & C. Van Velsen (Eds.), *A Practical Guide to Forensic Psychotherapy* (pp. 188–193). London:Jessica Kingsley.

Mitchell, J. (1997). Sexuality, psychoanalysis and social change. *IPA News Letter, 6*(1): 15–18.

Mitscherlich, A. (1963)[1970]. *Verso una società senza padre.* Milan: Feltrinelli.

Nathan, T. (1984). La transgression du tabou narcissique. Pris. Cahier U.E.R. *Experimentale de Bobigny, 24*: 51–61.

Pazzagli A. (1999). Il travaglio della paternità. In: S. Argentieri (Ed.), *Il padre materno. Da San Giuseppe ai nuovi mammi* (pp. 14–30). Rome: Meltemi.

Pine, F. (1999). Le quattro psicologie della psicoanalisi e il loro posto nel lavoro clinico. *Psicoanalisi, 3*(1): 311–318.

Pines, D. (1992). The relevance of early psychic development to pregnancy and abortion. *International Journal of Psycho-Analysis, 63*: 311–318.

Quallenberg, J. (2002). El refugio: una solución melancólica en un contexto de sumisión masoquista. Paper presented at the XLII Annual Congress of the Mexican Psychoanalytic Association, Guanajuato, November 2002.

Racamier, P.-C. (1995). *L'inceste et l'incestuel*. Paris: Les éditions du collège.

Rascovsky, A., & Wencelblat de Rascovsky, M. (1950). On consummated incest. *International Journal of Psychoanalysis*, *31*(1–2): 42–47.

Rosenberg, B. (1991). Masochisme mortifère et masochisme gardien de la vie. *Monographie de la Revue Française de Psychoanalyse*. Paris: PUF.

Sandler, J. (1983). Reflection on some relation between psychoanalytic concepts and psychoanalytic practice. *International Journal of Psycho-Analysis*, *64*: 35–46.

Sandler, J., & Fonagy, P. (Eds.) (1997). *Recovered Memories of Abuse: True or False?* London: Karnac.

Sant'Agostino (1963). *De Civitate Dei*. Rome: Edizioni Paoline.

Servadio, E. (1954). Prefazione a S. Freud, 1925, "Inibizione, sintomo e angoscia", pp. 7–17. Turin: Einaudi.

Shengold, L. (1980). Some reflections on a case of mother/adolescent son incest. *International Journal of Psychoanalysis*, *61*(4): 461–476.

Speziale Bagliacca, R. (1997). *Colpa*. Rome: Astrolabio Ubaldini.

Speziale Bagliacca, R. (2002). *Freud messo a fuoco*. Turin: Bollati Boringhieri.

Starke, C. N. (1888). *Die Primitive Familie*. Lipsia: Brockhaus.

Steiner, J. (1993). 'Due tipi di organizzazione patologica nell' "Edipo re"e nell' "Edipo a Colono". In: *I rifugi della mente*. Turin: Bollati Boringhieri. English edition (1993). Two types of pathological organization in *Oedipus the King* and *Oedipus at Colonus*. In: *Psychic Retreats* (pp. 116–130). London: Routledge.

Szpilka, J. (1985). Edipo precoce, effetto retroattivo e conflitto psichico. *Rivista di Psicoanalisi*, *XXXI*(5): 34–74.

Tesone, J. E. (1994). Notas psicoanalíticas sobre el incesto comsumado: el triángulo deshecho? *Revista de Psicología y Psicoterapia de Grupo*. *XVII*(1): 169–187, and in *PSYCHE* (1996). 9/10: 836–849.

Tylor, E. B. (1888). On a method of investigating the development of institutions. *Journal of the Royal Anthropological Institute*, *18*:

van der Kolk, B. (1989). The compulsion to repeat the trauma: re-enactment, re-victimisation and masochism. *Psychiat. Clin North Am.*, *12*: 389–411.

Vernant, J.-P. (1999). *L'univers, les dieux, les hommes*. Paris: Seuil. English edition: *The Universe, the Gods, and Men* (L. Asher, Trans.). London: Harper Collins (2001).

Welldon, E. V. (1991). A psychoanalytical viewpoint on feminine perversions. Freud Memorial Lecture, London University.

Welldon, E. V. (1997). *The Foulkes Lecture, Group Analysis* Vol. 30, pp. 9–26. Sage Publications.

Westermarck, E., (1894). *The History of Human Marriage*. London: Macmillan.

Winnicott, D. W. (1958). *Trough Paediatrics to Psychoanalysis*. London: Tavistock.

BIBLIOGRAPHY

Altan, C. T. (1971). *Manuale di antropologia culturale.* Milan: Bompiani.

Amati, J., Argentieri, S., & Canestri, J. (1993). *The Babel of the Unconscious: Mother Tongue and Foreign Languages in the Psychoanalytic Dimension.* Madison, CT: International Universities Press.

Ambrosio, G. (2002). La menzogna annunciata. *Psicoanalisi,* 6(1): 75–94.

Argentieri, S. (1982b). Anna Freud, la figlia. In: S. Vegetti Finzi (Ed.), *Psicoanalisi al femminile.* Rome: Laterza.

Argentieri, S. (2000). La malafede come nevrosi e come crimine. *Psicoanalisi,* 4(2): 157–171.

Barbagli, M. (1993). Voce "Famiglia", (1) sociologia. In: *Enciclopedia delle scienze sociali, vol. III.* Rome: Istituto della Enciclopedia Italiana Treccani.

Bion, W. R. (1991). *A Memoir of tha Future,* volumes 1–3. London: Karnac.

Britton, R. (1989). The missing link: parental sexuality in the Oedipus complex. In: J. Steiner (Ed.), *The Oedipus Complex Today.* London: Karnac.

Canestri, J. (1994). Alcune note sulla "formazione del padre" e i processi psicotici. In: M. L. Mascagni (Ed.), *Studi sul pensiero di Eugenio Gaddini* (pp. 172–180). Chieti: Metis.

Canestri, J. (1998). Psychoanalytic heuristics for psychoanalytic theories in practice: a Festschrift to Joseph Sandler. In: P. Fonagy, A. Cooper,

& R. Wallerstein (Eds.), *Psychoanalysis on the Move. The work of Joseph Sandler* (pp. 201–216). London: Routledge.

Carratelli, T. (1995). Padre e madre . . . in cerca di papà e mamma. In *Bollettino A.I.Psi.*, 3: 18–24.

Carratelli, T. (1995). Transfert e trasmissione della vita psichica tra generazioni, intervento alla "Tavola Rotonda" *Il mito di Edipo rivisitato del Convegno ASNE-SIPSIA*, 11 November, Rome.

Darwin, C. (1859). *The Origin of Species*, London:

Darwin, C. (1871) *The Descent of Man*. London.

Ferenczi, S. (1933)[1949]. Confusion of tongues between the adult and the child. (The language of tenderness and of passion). *International Journal of Psychoanalysis*, 30(IV): 225–230.

Frazer, J. G. (1910). *Totemism and Esogamy*. London.

Gaddini, E. (1989). *Scritti—1953–1985*. Milan: R. Cortina.

Grossmann, W. (2001). Presentazione del "modo psicoanalitico di pensare" di Freud in *Totem e tabù* e negli scritti sulla tecnica. *Psicoanalisi*, 5(2): 101–126.

Lévi-Strauss, C. (1958). *Anthropologie structurale*. Paris: Plon.

Lévi-Strauss, C. (1962). *Le totémisme aujourd'hui*. Paris: PUF.

Lowie, R. (1917). *Culture and Ethnology*. New York: D. C. McMurtrie.

Malinowski, B., 1944[1971], *Teoria scientifica della cultura e altri saggi*. Milan: Feltrinelli.

McLennan, J. F. (1896). *An Inquiry into the Origin of Exogamy*. London: Macmillan.

Mead, M. (1949). *Male and Female*. New York: W. Morrow.

Molfino, F. (1995). Seduzione del padre, seduzione della madre. In: *Corpo a corpo* (pp. 98–112). Bari: Laterza.

Sandler, J., & Sandler, A.-M. (1983). The second censorship, the three box model and some technical implication. *International Journal of Psycho-Analysis*, 64: 413–425.

Tesone, J. E. (1996). L'inceste: le triangle défait. *Revista de Psicologia y psicoterapia de Grupo, Buenos Aires 1994.* e in *Psyche*, 9/10, Stuttgart.

Tesone, J. E. (1998). Une activité peu masculine: l'inceste père—fille, *Revue Francaise de Psychanalyse*, LXII(2): 513–525.

Tesone, J. E. (2001). De la théorie de la séduction à la séduction traumatique: l'inceste. Workshop, 42nd IPA Conference, Nice.

Welldon, E. V. (1988). *Mother, Madonna, Whore: The Idealisation and Denigration of Motherhood*. Free Association Books, [reprinted New York: Guilford Press, 1992].

Zucconi, S. (2002) L'Edipo oggi. *Psicoanalisi*, 6(1): 95–108.